MW00461898

"Prof. Mellott's book addresses tw
in theology—What can we, the 'pr
and Christian lives? What can they
missed? Focusing on the religious
Mellott discovers challenging and deeply spiritual ways of knowing that
should affect the way all Christian theology is crafted today. Reading this
excellent book confirms once again that theologians need to pay close
methodological attention to the faith of the people."

> —*Orlando Espín*
> *Professor of Systematic Theology*
> *Director of the Center for the Study of Latino/a Catholicism*
> *University of San Diego*

"An accomplished storyteller, David Mellott gives us two things at once:
a vivid narrative and a pointed lesson. His narrative seeks out the rituals,
memories, and visions of penitente life in northern New Mexico. His lesson is
that there can be no liturgical theology—no theology at all—without listening
to particular lives as if they really might have something to tell us."

> —*Mark D. Jordan*
> *Harvard Divinity School*

"In clear and compelling prose, David Mellott narrates his ethnographic
encounter with the Penitente Hermanos of Arroyo Seco, New Mexico.
Mellott's account conveys the breath-taking intensity of the group's public
spiritual dramas as well as the poignancy of personal stories of struggle and
renewal. What does it mean to be dust? To know one's self? Mellott draws
readers in to these questions, even as he opens out the particular history and
practices of the Hermandad. Students and scholars, liturgists and laity will
appreciate this sparkling text, in which ethnography—'a form of prayerful
beholding and attentiveness'—becomes theology."

> —*Mary Clark Moschella*
> *Wesley Theological Seminary*
> *Author of* Ethnography as a Pastoral Practice: An Introduction

The Virgil Michel Series

Virgil Michel, OSB, a monk of Saint John's Abbey in Collegeville, Minnesota, was a founder of the Liturgical Movement in the United States in the 1920s and fostered its development until his death in 1938. Michel's writing, editing, teaching, and preaching centered on the relationship between liturgy and the life of the faithful—the Body of Christ.

The Pueblo Books imprint of Liturgical Press honors Virgil Michel's life and work with a monograph series named for him. The Virgil Michel Series will offer studies that examine the connections between liturgy and life in particular communities, as well as works exploring the relationship of liturgy to theology, ethics, and social sciences. The Virgil Michel Series will be ecumenical in breadth and international in scope, recognizing that liturgy embodies yet transcends cultures and denominations.

Series Editor: Don E. Saliers

Don E. Saliers, who teaches regularly at Saint John's University, is the William R. Cannon Distinguished Professor of Theology and Worship, emeritus, at Emory University, Atlanta, Georgia.

David M. Mellott

I Was
and
I Am Dust

Penitente Practices
as a Way of Knowing

Virgil Michel Series

Don E. Saliers, Editor

A PUEBLO BOOK

Liturgical Press   Collegeville, Minnesota

www.litpress.org

A Pueblo Book published by Liturgical Press

Cover design by David Manahan, OSB. Cover art by Larry T. Torres. See pages 145–46 for description.

Library of Congress Cataloging-in-Publication Data

Mellott, David M.
    I was and I am dust : penitente practices as a way of knowing / David M. Mellott ; Don E. Saliers, editor.
        p.   cm.—(The Virgil Michel series)
    "A Pueblo book."
    Includes bibliographical references and index.
    ISBN 978-0-8146-6225-0
    1. Spiritual life—Catholic Church.   2. Candles and lights.   3. Flagellation.
4. Hermanos Penitentes.   I. Saliers, Don E., 1937–   II. Title.

BX2350.3M45 2009
267'.242789—dc22   2009023184

Contents

Foreword   vii
   by Don E. Saliers

Preface   ix

Acknowledgments   xv

Introduction   1

Chapter 1. Historical Background   21

Chapter 2. Holy Week in Arroyo Seco   41

Chapter 3. Era y soy polvo   67

Chapter 4. Ethnography as Theology   91

Appendix 1. The Feast Day of Nuestra Señora de los Dolores   115

Appendix 2. The First Night of Las Posadas   123

Appendix 3. Larry Torres' Life Stories   131

Appendix 4. Larry's Picture Book   149

Select Bibliography   155

Index   159

The Penitente Paintings by Isaac L. Udell   167

Foreword

It is difficult now to believe that theological thinking about sacraments could proceed for so long without paying attention to the details of liturgical life. It would be difficult to understand how religious communities understand themselves theologically without studying how persons actually live and practice their faith. Thus it is significant that theologians have increasingly turned toward the actual practices of religious communities for insight into what and how people make sense of their religious life. In recent decades a growing literature focusing on the varied devotional, liturgical, and ritual practices of daily life has begun to open up deeper connections between human experience and theological insight. How is the Christian life really lived and interpreted? What can Christian theology learn from detailed observation and conversations with living groups of Christians? These questions animate David Mellott's pages.

This book makes an impressive case for ethnographic study of particular communal practices as a major contribution to theological studies. It does so by taking us deeply into the Holy Week rituals of the Penitentes of Arroyo Seco, New Mexico. Very few readers will know much about the Brotherhood and its seemingly off-putting practice of flagellation and ritual identification with the passion of Christ. Yet, as we are taken inside this community, we may begin to appreciate what Aidan Kavanagh and others have called "primary theology"—what is transacted and enacted between God and human beings in actual ritual and life practices.

I am especially pleased that this study appears in the Virgil Michel Series. David Mellott's book offers an uncommonly forged depiction of what few have been privileged to see and hear. While its subject is an uncommon Christian community, such a depiction reveals what theology often misses in our tendencies to abstract from the specificity of the theological depth of the whole pattern of a faith community's life and struggles.

The reader comes away from these pages with a more profound appreciation for the rich layering of meaning-making and depth of spirituality found in the Morada of Arroyo Seco. David Mellott's deep respect and empathy as well as his descriptive acuity are found in every phase of this study. This book stands robustly at the intersection of ethnographic study and theological reflection on matters of life and death—the mystery of Christ's passion and its reception in particular cultural forms.

Don E. Saliers

Preface

In the early 1990s I served as associate pastor for a Roman Catholic Church in the Midwest. Our parish literally sold truckloads of votive candles each year despite the best efforts of the pastoral staff to discourage the practice by removing or relocating the candle stands and by (re)labeling the custom as "superstitious." On numerous occasions we had to unlock the church doors at odd hours so that a parishioner could light a candle in church and pray for the needs of a friend or family member.

One particular Sunday evening we received a call in the rectory from Mary Elizabeth, one of our elderly members. Mary Elizabeth asked me if I would reopen the church so that she could light an eight-day votive candle for the safety of her granddaughter, who was leaving for Paris the next morning. I gently suggested that Mary Elizabeth could say a prayer at home for her granddaughter and that she could light the candle the following morning when she came for daily Mass. Mary Elizabeth insisted that the candle needed to be lit that night. She had promised her granddaughter that the candle would be burning when she flew to Paris early the next morning. In the end, Mary Elizabeth agreed that it would be satisfactory for me to light the candle for her and place it on the Marian side altar; she would offer the prayer for the safe travels of her granddaughter from her home.

When I returned to the rectory after lighting the candle for her, the other members of the pastoral team questioned me about the wisdom of my decision to light the candle for her. They wanted to know why I was helping her. According to them, instead of lighting the votive candle for her, I should have used the opportunity to explain to her that lighting votive candles is a superstitious practice that encourages an immature relationship with God. I understood what they were saying. In fact, I agreed with them that God didn't need a votive candle to be lit in order to hear Mary Elizabeth's prayer for her granddaughter. I also shared their concern about the quality of Mary Elizabeth's spiritual development. Like them, I was taught that many of the pre-Vatican II practices in the Roman Catholic Church supported a less developed faith that often manifested itself in the striving of human beings to manipulate God. Unlike them, however, I grew up after the reforms of the Second Vatican Council had been implemented. I also grew up in a family that did not engage in the practice of lighting votive candles. I tried to invite Mary Elizabeth to consider the possibility that God would hear her prayer without lighting the votive candle. Because she wasn't open to my perspective at that moment I decided not to stand in the way of her spiritual practice. At our next staff meeting, however, we decided to renew our commitment to teaching the parishioners about the dangers of superstitious spiritual practices.

Years later I reflected on those particular interactions with Mary Elizabeth and our pastoral team. Only then did I realize that it never occurred to us to invite Mary Elizabeth, or any of the other dozens of parishioners who were like her, into a conversation about their spiritual practices and what they meant to them. Asking them about their experiences and the ways they understood their practices didn't occur to us because we assumed that we knew more about their practices than they did. Even though we did not participate in the practice of lighting votive candles, we had concluded that it was a practice indicative of an immature faith. Furthermore, we could cite the testimony of expert theologians and psychologists who had published books and journal articles about levels of psychological development and the spiritual practices that correspond with each of the stages.

We didn't need to talk with Mary Elizabeth; there wasn't anything she could tell us that was worth knowing. At least that was what I thought then. Now I realize that I missed a valuable opportunity to hear her stories about how she lived her faith and how her practice of lighting votive candles, among other practices, shaped her life of faith. Even worse, I lost the chance to allow her stories and her life to shape my life and my theology; I missed the chance for a deeper spiritual relationship with Mary Elizabeth.

Today, many years later, I remain fascinated by the dynamic that was occurring between our parish staff and our votive-candle-lighting congregants. The practice of lighting votive candles makes sense to me in the pre–Vatican II era, when the communal nature of the Eucharist was obscured and church law closely regulated spiritual practices. Lighting votive candles was one of few things that Catholic laypeople could do without permission or much interference from the clergy. All the members of our staff, however, were strong promoters of the reforms of the Second Vatican Council. We preached and taught that the work of the church was the work of all the people, clergy, religious, and laity. We wanted our parishioners to trade in their votive candles for an active role in the eucharistic assembly. The irony was that we were still dictating what people should do and how they should interpret what they were doing. We claimed that the people were primary actors in the life of the church, but we didn't treat them as such. If we had, we would have engaged them in conversation about their practices and we would have paid closer attention to the ways in which those practices shaped their faith. If we had chosen to interact with them on that level, I suspect we would have also been challenged to be more aware and forthcoming about our own anxieties, concerns, and doubts that lingered within our own spiritual practices. Our exchanges might not have ended in agreement, but they would have strengthened the bonds among us. We also would have learned something theological from these practitioners.

As popular as votive candle lighting has remained among Roman Catholics, despite heavy scrutiny and criticism since the Second Vatican Council, conceiving that we could learn something theological from the people who have been engaging it, often for decades, allowed me to imagine learning from Roman Catholics who engage in less popular and more extreme forms of spiritual practice.[1] Imagine, now, conversing with a member of a church-sanctioned, voluntary fraternity of Roman Catholics who strip down to their underwear, press their faces into a dirt floor, and beat themselves with a whip of cactus fibers to the point of bleeding. Larry T. Torres, a Roman Catholic layman, has performed this penitential practice for over four decades as part of his membership in the Penitentes, which means "penitent ones" in Spanish. He joined the fraternity of Penitentes in northern New Mexico when he was nine years old. This book is an exploration of his experiences.

Despite the fact that many books have been written about the Penitentes in the United States and other countries, few Christians, including Roman Catholics, are familiar with this penitential practice. Flagellation, the act of scourging oneself or being scourged,

---

[1] I find this idea exciting. Others, however, are less enthusiastic. Once, while speaking with a diocesan director of religious education, she told me that it was ridiculous to ask Roman Catholics about their experience with lighting votive candles, praying the rosary, or any other devotion. For her, the church's teaching had made it clear that the Eucharist was the central practice for Roman Catholics. She thought that my idea to ask Roman Catholics about their experiences was not only a waste of time, but also "not very Catholic."

however, is a practice that has been used for spiritual purposes for centuries. Upon first hearing about this practice, we may find it hard to imagine why someone would voluntarily beat oneself and why the Roman Catholic Church would approve of a behavior that causes such physical pain. As extreme as this spiritual practice is, we may not assume that we know more about it than Larry and his fellow practitioners, but we may assume that we know enough to say that the practice couldn't lead to any spiritual wisdom. From a distance, some of us may quickly charge that the practice is dangerous, physically and psychologically, and it has no place within the Christian community. That was certainly my concern when I first learned about the Penitentes in New Mexico. Supporting my assumptions was the fact that Pope Pius IX had ordered the disbandment of the fraternity in the nineteenth century.

What if, however, we were to take the time to ask Larry about his experience? What if we asked him about what he has learned from doing this practice for the last four decades? What if we could spend long periods of time with him, talking with him and following him around as he went about his daily life, to see how his experience of being a Penitente shapes who he is and his understanding of the spiritual life? Most of us would be surprised by what we would learn. I was. Through his participation in flagellation and the other practices of the Penitentes, Larry has found a way to a deeper knowledge of himself, God, and the world. He has come to know that he was and he is dust; an insight that has given him new life. In fact, his communion with the dust of the earth has been more powerful to him than the "ecstasies" of receiving Communion at Mass.

This book was born out of my experiment with finding out what I could learn from Larry and his experience of Penitente spirituality, including flagellation. The process was more challenging than I had imagined. My theological training didn't prepare me to consider what laypeople could teach me, especially about theology or spirituality. I had to set aside my assumptions that I knew more than Larry and the other Penitentes about their practices and what counted as an acceptable spiritual practice within the Christian tradition.

In the pages that follow you are invited to join me in my process of trying to understand Larry and the Penitentes of northern New Mexico on their own terms. My intention is not to convince you to become a Penitente. I do hope that what you learn about Larry's experience and my experience of seeking to understand him better will inspire you to go out and engage the Larrys and Mary Elizabeths in your world. I suspect you will be surprised by what you hear and see. I imagine that you will not only learn about them, their experiences, and their world, but also about yourself, your assumptions, and the life you are creating.

Acknowledgments

Selecting a research project and then bringing it to completion can be a perilous process. Fortunately, my decision to research the practices of the Penitentes in Arroyo Seco, New Mexico, was greeted with enthusiasm from many of my professors at Emory University, where I did my research and writing. In particular, I am grateful to Don Saliers, whose passionate interest in my work and wise counsel carried me through many difficult moments in the writing process. Joyce Flueckiger and Mark Jordan graciously guided me through the process of bringing theology and ethnography together. Joyce patiently mentored me as I ventured into ethnographic research. Mark gently and persistently helped me to see the wider implications of bringing together ethnographic research and theology. I also benefited from my conversations with Bobbie Patterson, Wendy Farley, Nancy Eiesland, and Brian Mahan while working on this project.

Early on in the research stage, Robert Orsi advised me to "always tell the truth" in the research process. This advice and his ongoing support of this project sustained me despite the many changes in my personal life while doing my research and the writing.

The financial support of the Graduate Division of Religion at Emory, the Society of St. Sulpice, and the Louisville Institute made my fieldwork in Arroyo Seco possible. The generosity of family members and friends was also significant in bringing this project to completion.

I am indebted to several other people who assisted, guided, and inspired me during the writing stages of this project. I am particularly grateful to Helen Mitchell, my friend and former colleague at Howard Community College, whose willingness to think with me about the writing process allowed my voice to emerge. Jeremy Paden and Nasario García helped in creating the English translations of the sacred dramas of the Penitentes. Fran Kelleher saved me from becoming isolated through my work and was the perfect writing partner and friend.

Although the initial draft of this manuscript was written during my graduate studies at Emory University, I revised and prepared the final text for publication with Liturgical Press after I began teaching at Lancaster Theological Seminary. I am grateful to my students in the Doctor of Ministry program who closely read and commented on some of the chapters. Their comments helped me to clarify my thoughts, and their delight in ethnographic research motivated me to get this manuscript published. Bryce Rich, a staff member of our library and one of my students, offered much-needed and appreciated assistance in preparing the electronic files of the Udell paintings.

From the moment of my initial interview at the seminary, I have been deeply grateful for the enthusiasm the seminary faculty has shown for my research and writing. Thanks to my colleagues I have been given the freedom to explore with our students the ways ethnographic research can enrich programmatic theological education. I am grateful to Ed Aponte, our dean, who regularly advised me to make room in my schedule for writing. In addition, Bruce Epperly and Bud Hartley provided valuable comments on early drafts of the manuscript. Anabel Proffitt and Julia O'Brien helped me to remember the gift and pleasure of writing.

Hans Christoffersen, editorial director at Liturgical Press, and Don Saliers, editor of the Virgil Michel Series, have been guiding forces as I transformed my doctoral dissertation into the current book. Mary Stommes, Lauren L. Murphy, Colleen Stiller, and Ann Blattner, also at Liturgical Press, patiently guided me through the editorial process and helped tremendously to create a more readable text. I am honored by Liturgical Press's decision to include *I Was and I Am Dust* in the Virgil Michel Series. The editorial staff's excitement about the book nourished my own enthusiasm for bringing theology and ethnography together.

To the members of Holy Trinity Parish in Arroyo Seco, New Mexico, I owe a special word of gratitude. They generously welcomed me into the life of their community. To all those who invited me to participate with them in their activities and to those who spoke with me about their experiences, I am very grateful. I especially want to thank Rev. Vincent Chávez, who invited me to Arroyo Seco the first time and who introduced me to the Penitentes. Most of all, I want to thank Larry Torres, whose participation made my research possible and provocative. His remarkable openness transformed me and my appreciation for the potential of ethnographic research. I look forward to many more years of working together with him. Special words of gratitude go to Tina Larkin of *The Taos News*, who provided the photograph of Larry's painting *Era y Soy Polvo* for the front cover.

Thanks to the permission of Farrell Udell and Christy Udell Stripe, son and daughter of Isaac L. Udell, I have been able to include in this book Isaac's thirteen Penitente paintings. These paintings have never been published in color and are a valuable part of the history of the Penitentes in New Mexico. I am honored that the Udell family and the owner of the collection entrusted me with the publication of these works of art.

Through the unfolding of this project I have enjoyed the immeasurable support of family and friends. My parents, Joyce and Francis Mellott, were the ones who taught me to listen to the stories of others. Sharon and Joseph Mellott, my sister and brother, never tired of reassuring me of my potential. Mary Mellott, Kurt Ewen, Joe Reynolds, Gaila Mullins, Terry Mullins, Pauline Gurley, Patrice Miles, and Jesse Miles regularly offered encouragement, especially in my moments of frustration and disappointment.

Most important, my life partner, Lance Mullins, has been my best friend and my delight throughout this creative and challenging adventure. His love and laughter have nourished me. His wise counsel and his commitment to the ways of Jesus have helped me to discover my voice and my path in this world.

February 2, 2009
The Feast of the Presentation of Jesus

Introduction

From the mid-1980s to the early 1990s I studied theology at one of
the oldest Roman Catholic universities in the world: the Katholieke
Universiteit Leuven (KUL) in Belgium. Fresh from college seminary
in the United States, I went to Leuven to study theology at the fa-
mous university and to prepare to become a Roman Catholic priest.
My classes at the KUL included students from around the world who
were also preparing to become priests or professional theologians or
both. During our first semester of theological studies we noticed that
the professors would lecture all three hours of our class time. No time
was allotted for questions, comments, or discussion with the professor
or our classmates. We soon realized that this was the teaching phi-
losophy behind the classes that we were taking there. Attending class
meant listening to the lecture and adding any additional comments
to the preprinted sets of notes we had purchased from the bookstore.
The classroom dynamics were never explained to us by the professors.
Consequently, we looked to upper-level students to inform us about
why we weren't allowed, or at least encouraged, to ask questions at
the end of a lecture or to engage the professor in a conversation. Our
informants interpreted the pedagogical practice as the professors' way
of communicating to us that we were not in a position to ask questions
or to have a conversation with them because we didn't know anything
about theology yet. We didn't have anything to contribute to a theological conversation. Our informants also explained that if we continued into the second cycle of theological studies (beyond the three-year
bachelor program), the professors would begin to accept questions
and permit some discussion at the end of class.

My formation as a theologian and pastoral minister left a strong
impression on my self-understanding. I saw myself as an expert when
I arrived as a priest in the parish and as a professor in the classroom.
The fact that I received both the training to be a professional theologian and a pastoral minister enhanced this image I had of myself. I
became dedicated to passing on the valuable information that was
passed on to me. In fact, at the beginning of my first assignment as

a priest, the pastor asked me if I would be willing to take over the weekly column in the church bulletin, titled "Did You Know?" which had been written by the former assistant pastor.

I offer this narrative because it unmasks some of the assumptions embedded in the patterns of my formation as a professional theologian and pastoral minister. Among those assumptions were that I arrived at the university with no knowledge of theology, and that when I graduated, I would be an expert in theology. The pedagogical practices of that theological studies program were geared toward providing me with all the knowledge I needed to become an expert in theology. The hope was that I would go forth from the university and pass on that knowledge to the people in my parishes and my classrooms who were similarly uneducated. I was charged to tell them what we assumed they didn't know.

The assumption that the people in our parishes and classrooms were uneducated theologically went beyond their not knowing the details of church history, Scripture, liturgy, and systematic theology. The assumption was that because the people didn't know these important pieces of information, they couldn't make any sense out of what we were doing as a faith community. More specifically, many of my colleagues and I believed that people weren't able to interpret the liturgical practices of the community, or even their own individual spiritual practices, because they didn't know the history, development, and church codes that were associated with those practices.

My assumptions about being an expert in theology, however, were quickly challenged by the people in our church and the students in my classroom. For example, no matter how many times a member of the parish staff or a faculty colleague would explain that the Second Vatican Council stated clearly in the Constitution on the Liturgy that the liturgy was the source and the summit of the life of the church and that full, active participation in the liturgy was expected,[1] people would continue to pray the rosary during Mass. Their persistent resistance to our teachings and mandates intrigued me. I began to question whether I was an expert, and whether the people in my parish had something to teach me.

---

[1] The Constitution on the Liturgy (*Sacrosanctum Concilium*) can be found in *Documents on the Liturgy 1963–1979: Conciliar, Papal, and Curial Texts*, ed. International Committee on English in the Liturgy (Collegeville, MN: Liturgical Press, 1982) as DOL 1.

RAISING THE QUESTION

Is there anything we—theologians and pastoral ministers—can *learn* by asking our Christian companions about their everyday lives, about what they consider to be their spiritual practices, and about the ways in which they understand and interpret those practices in the midst of their contexts?[2] Yes, there is much of considerable importance we can learn from studying the lived experience of practicing Christians. The underlying argument of this book is that ethnographic research should be an essential component of theological studies. I have chosen to make this argument primarily through performing ethnographic research and sharing my results and reflections in written form. Another argument of this book comes from what I learned in the process of doing ethnographic research in Arroyo Seco, New Mexico: doing ethnographic research can also be a theological act.

Through extended interviewing, participant observation, and gathering spiritual life stories, I explored the practices of the Penitente Brotherhood performed in the northern New Mexican village of Arroyo Seco and how those practices have been experienced by one of their most senior members. The most commonly used formal name for the Brotherhood is La Fraternidad Piadosa de Nuestro Padre Jesús Nazareno.[3] More popularly, they are known as Penitentes (Penitent Ones) or Hermanos (Brothers) or la Hermandad (the Brotherhood).[4] They have established a number of chapters, called Moradas, throughout northern New Mexico and southern Colorado.

Throughout this inquiry the reader will notice that I have chosen to capitalize all references to the Brothers, the Moradas, and the Brotherhood as a whole. I have done so because those terms were presented

---

[2] Although the context of my question and my research is the Roman Catholic Church, I have chosen to use the terms "Christian" and "pastoral minister" because I believe other denominations would also benefit from engaging this question.

[3] The Pious Fraternity of Our Father Jesus of Nazareth.

[4] In at least one other village, the members use other titles. Nuestra Señora de Guadalupe Morada uses the word Cofradía (Confraternity), instead of Fraternidad (Fraternity). In addition, they use Cofrados and Cofradas to refer to the men and women who belong to their Morada. They use this language intentionally to reflect the presence of men and women in their Morada. See Felipe Ortega's foreword to Michael Wallis and Craig Varjabedian, *En Divina Luz: The Penitente Moradas of New Mexico* (Albuquerque: University of New Mexico Press, 1994), xiii.

this way in the local parish bulletins and newspaper columns I read. Customarily, in English-language documents, words from other languages are italicized. I have chosen not to italicize the Spanish words, however, because they are not considered foreign words to the people of this community. Local parish bulletins and publications, which utilize both the Spanish and English languages, do not italicize Spanish words.

SITUATING THE QUESTION

My proposal that theologians and pastoral ministers should inquire into the spiritual practices of fellow Christians and engage them in conversation about how they interpret those practices is not particularly new. Aidan Kavanagh made a similar suggestion in 1981, in his Hale Memorial Lectures of Seabury-Western Theological Seminary. In his lectures, which were recast into his manifesto, *On Liturgical Theology*, Kavanagh challenges the way in which theology has been practiced and understood within the academy. He claims that thinking about God and about humanity's relationship with God has become primary in theological studies. Consequently, the actual being in relationship with God has become secondary. Yet, this is the place where humanity is changed, even if imperceptibly, through its encounter with God. Primary theology has shifted from *being in* relationship to *thinking about* that relationship. This shift, or better this reversal, has resulted in a diminished sense of both liturgical worship and theological reflection. First of all, theological reflection, or theologizing has been severed from its liturgical roots and is often lost in its desire for internal coherence and consistency. Second, liturgical worship has not only lost its place at the center of theology but also become the vehicle or tool by which doctrines can be promulgated and dispersed.

Against these tendencies, Kavanagh proposes that liturgical worship is primary Christian theology. Christian liturgy is the faith of the church in action. To put it another way, the celebration of the liturgy is a theological act. Kavanagh wishes to restore liturgical worship to its primacy within Christian theology. He develops his argument out of and around the patristic aphorism, *lex supplicandi legem statuat credendi*: the law of supplicating (praying) constitutes the law of believing (Prosper of Aquitane).[5] What Kavanagh doesn't acknowledge in his

---

[5] Prosper of Aquitane was a disciple of Augustine. For more on his perspective, including the connection with Augustine, see Basil Studer, "Liturgy and the Fathers," trans. Edward Hagman, in Anscar J. Chupungco, ed., *Introduction*

analysis of this maxim is that there are other examples of the faith of the church in action. Feeding the poor, clothing the naked, forgiving our enemies, and loving our neighbor as ourselves are also examples of faith in action. They are theological acts that also transform us through our encounter with God and one another.

Kavanagh proposes that the liturgy needs to be taken from the hands of liturgists, religious bureaucrats, and other specialists and returned to the people. When he says this, he is not talking about getting laypeople more involved in liturgical planning. What he envisions is an epistemological shift from the perspective of the specialists to that of the participants, and a shift in focus from the classroom and library to the field. A consequence of this restoration is that the people who participate in the liturgical life of the church are once again understood as primary theologians. These primary theologians know the liturgy through their participation in it. As an illustration of his point, Kavanagh gives an example of a group of tourists watching a group of New Mexican Indians perform a ritual dance. Kavanagh suggests that although the tourists may know a lot of facts about the ritual dances from the books they've read, they don't know the dances in the same way that the Indians know them. In the ecology of the academy, including theology, Kavanagh observes, ironically, that the interpretation of the tourists is more trustworthy than that of the dancers.[6] At the end of the first half of his argument, Kavanagh writes,

> I hoped to set up a situation in which alternatives might stand out in high contrast—such as World, City, and Church as artifacts, as things we make. I tried to seduce us all into artistic discourse, into talking and thinking about how we make and, in making, discover reality. If we could grow ourselves into that discovered reality, I suggested we might stumble onto the road out of suburbia, a road best traveled not in a tour bus but on foot so that we could stop when we wished in cold woods, with laughing flesh, to admire ladies in silk dresses and their beaux, and even get ourselves swept up into a rowdy mob on its way

to the Liturgy, vol. 1, _Handbook for Liturgical Studies_ (Collegeville, MN: Liturgical Press, 1997), 53–79, esp., 60–63.

[6] Aidan Kavanagh, _On Liturgical Theology: The Hale Memorial Lectures of Seabury-Western Theological Seminary, 1981_ (Collegeville, MN: Liturgical Press, 1984), 10.

downtown to do the world now and then, there perhaps to encounter a new possibility leaning into the wind.[7]

Despite Kavanagh's proposal to theologians and pastoral ministers nearly twenty-five years ago to hit the streets and to find out what Christians are doing, how they are doing it, and what they are discovering in the doing, few have taken up the challenge. This has been the case for several reasons. We'll discuss some of those reasons in chapter 4. For now it is sufficient to say that restoring the worship of the Christian community to its place of primacy within Christian theology is not enough. Attention must be given to how the assembly construes and deepens its own experience of the liturgy.

As I illustrated in the preface and in the narrative at the opening of this introduction, there has been and continues to be a presumption that there is little to be learned by paying attention to the lived experience of the members of the Christian community. When I was ordained a Roman Catholic priest in 1992, I was comfortable, perhaps too comfortable, with my new role as spiritual guide and authority. My formation as a priest and theologian included both studying the liturgical, theological, and pastoral reforms of the Second Vatican Council and living them. My classmates and I went into ministry with the charge to put into practice the vision put forth in the Constitution on the Liturgy: "every liturgical celebration, because it is an action of Christ the Priest and of his Body which is the Church, is a sacred action surpassing all others; no other action of the Church can equal its effectiveness by the same title and to the same degree" (SC 7). The liturgy of the church was to be central in my life as a priest and in the lives of the Roman Catholics that I served. There was no need to inquire among our parishioners about their spiritual practices and what they meant to them. Our responsibility as pastoral ministers was to teach them which practices should be central in their lives. More important, we were to teach them what those practices were supposed to mean to them.

Talking about practicing Christians as primary theologians is very different from treating them as primary theologians. Historians of religion, sociologists, anthropologists, and a few theologians are out in the field, in our communities, seeking to understand more fully the lived experience of Christians. Many of them are employing ethnographic

[7] Ibid., 69.

6

research methods, such as participant observation, interviews, focus groups, life stories, and surveys, to gather their information. They are studying Christians who are handling snakes,[8] flagellating themselves,[9] seeking the intervention of a particular saint in heaven,[10] or who have a relationship with and devotion to Mary through a specific apparition.[11] These are just a few examples of the research that is taking place within Christian communities. Robert Orsi laments they are too few, that little attention is paid to the "experiences and beliefs of people in the midst of their lives," in both religious studies and theological studies. Orsi writes:

> Flushing with pride edged by anger, I think: I am here among these working-class people in this postindustrial landscape because I want to hear their stories. I take their voices seriously. This is what research in religion means, I fume, to attend to the experiences and beliefs of people in the midst of their lives, to encounter religion in its place in actual men and women's lived experience, in the places where they live and work. Where are the theologians from the seminaries on the South Side, I want to know, with all their talk of postmodernism and narrativity? When will the study of religion in the United States take an empirical and so more realistic and humane direction?[12]

Christian theologians need to pay more attention to practicing Christians and the everyday circumstances of their lives. Ethnographic research can help us do that.

Let me be clear here about a few things that I am not suggesting. I am not suggesting that Christian theologians, pastoral ministers,

---

[8] See Dennis Covington, *Salvation on Sand Mountain: Snake Handling and Redemption in Southern Appalachia* (Reading, MA: Addison-Wesley, 1995), as noted in Robert Orsi, *Between Heaven and Earth: The Religious Worlds People Make and the Scholars Who Study Them* (Princeton, NJ: Princeton University Press, 2005), 238.

[9] See Michael P. Carroll, *The Penitente Brotherhood: Patriarchy and Hispano-Catholicism in New Mexico* (Baltimore, MD: Johns Hopkins University Press, 2002).

[10] See Robert Orsi, *Thank You, St. Jude: Women's Devotion to the Patron Saint of Hopeless Causes* (New Haven, CT: Yale University Press, 1996).

[11] See Jeanette Rodríquez, *Our Lady of Guadalupe: Faith and Empowerment among Mexican-American Women* (Austin: University of Texas Press, 1994).

[12] Orsi, *Between Heaven and Earth*, 147.

or, more specifically, liturgical theologians go out on reconnaissance missions to learn how people respond to particular practices in their various styles, shapes, and techniques, so that they can in turn plan more effective liturgies and rituals. Nor am I suggesting that we explore the everyday circumstances of Christians so that we'll be better equipped to guide them toward the official, authorized rituals of our particular denominations. I am not advocating another method by which we can simply gather more data about Christians and the way they live, organize, and interpret their lives. And, I am certainly not advocating ethnographic research as a way for theologians and pastoral ministers to arrive at a definitive interpretation of why a particular group of people perform a particular practice (e.g., why some Roman Catholics have a devotion to the Divine Mercy) in order to put a particular practice (and its practitioners) into our established categories or hierarchies of religious experience.[13] In fact, one thing that ethnographic research helps display is the multiple and multifaceted ways in which people interpret what they do. The working assumption is that there will be a variety of responses, positions, and interpretations among a group of participants.

I am suggesting that we take seriously the peoples' experiences of being primary theologians. Ethnographic research can provide theologians and pastoral ministers with an opportunity to *learn* about the practices the people are doing, how they are doing them, and what those practices mean to them. Through this type of research we will also be able to better appreciate the multiple ways in which people engage and interpret their religious practices. This is not as simple as it may sound. As researchers we can be tempted to think that all people who participate in a particular practice or share in an event will have the same experience or the same self-understanding.

Beyond learning about other Christians, doing ethnographic research provides a structure through which the researcher can enter

---

[13] I am thinking here specifically of the way in which Erik Erikson's work on the ontogeny of ritualization, as found in *Identity, Youth, and Crisis* (Austen Briggs Monograph, no. 7 [New York: W. W. Norton, 1968]), was used in my courses on Roman Catholic liturgy as a way to categorize particular rituals or practices according to Erikson's levels of human development. Another book used to support the process of categorization was George S. Worgul Jr., *From Magic to Metaphor: A Validation of the Christian Sacraments* (New York: Paulist Press, 1980).

into relationship with the practitioners. In this case, when we are talking about Christian theologians and pastoral ministers going to other Christians to learn from them about the different ways they construct their lives and give them meaning, we are strengthening the bonds within the Christian body. Entering into relationship with other Christians in this way will require something of us. As we will see in chapters 3 and 4, we may be challenged by the ways we are both like and not like the people with whom we are working.

So far I have been using the term "theologian(s)" without explanation. Before proceeding any further I should clarify what I mean. Since I am using Kavanagh's work as a context for posing my question, I am also borrowing his terms of primary theologians and secondary theologians. By primary theologians he is referring to all members of the worshiping community. Through their participation in the worship of the church, they become primary theologians. The worship of the church community is the context for their relationship with God and one another. Secondary theologians are those we know more commonly in the academy and the church as "theologians." Their role is to reflect critically on this interaction between God and the worshiping community. Kavanagh writes, "For if theology as a whole is critical reflection upon the communion between God and our race, the peculiarly graced representative and servant of cosmic order created by God and restored in Christ, then scrutiny of the precise point at which this communion is most overtly deliberated upon and celebrated by us under God's judgment and in God's presence would seem to be crucial to the whole enterprise."[14] Throughout this book I will be using the terms "theologian" or "professional theologian" to designate those who provide that "critical reflection upon the communion between God and our race." At the same time, I consider the members of the community to be the primary theologians. The obvious problem with these terms is that they gloss over the fact that many, if not most, secondary theologians are also primary theologians, that is, they are worshipers too.

Before proceeding I want to address another possible concern: this type of research could be construed as condoning or approving particular practices and perspectives. On this matter I would agree with Orsi, who writes:

---

[14] Kavanagh, *On Liturgical Theology*, 78.

We may not condone or celebrate the religious practices of others—and let me emphasize this here because it is always misunderstood: to work toward some understanding(s) of troubling religious phenomena is not to endorse or sanction them . . . —but we cannot dismiss them as inhuman, so alien to us that they cannot be understood or approached, only contained or obliterated (which is what the language of good/bad religion accomplishes, the obliteration of the other by desire, need, or fear). The point is rather to bring the other into fuller focus within the circumstances of his or her history, relationships, and experiences. It is chastening and liberating to stand in an attitude of disciplined openness and attentiveness before a religious practice or idea or another era or culture on which we do not impose our wishes, dreams, or anxieties.[15]

Taking on this attitude of seeking to understand the religious practices of others without the intention of offering a final word on whether such behaviors are "appropriate," "healthy," or "Christian," may be extremely challenging for some theologians and even more pastoral ministers. While I know this can raise issues of ecclesiology and church polity I simply want to point out that practicing "disciplined openness and attentiveness" can become a kind of spiritual practice for the professional theologian or pastor. Furthermore, in particular situations, where there has been an expressed desire to "contain" or "obliterate" a set of practices by church authorities, as was the case with the Penitentes, researchers may find research participants especially hesitant about speaking with researchers who are associated with those authorities. It's in these very cases, however, where I think that ethnographic research can become a powerful theological act. Engaging people within their own contexts can create and strengthen relationships. We may find a particular practice to be troubling; if so, we are presented with an opportunity to learn how others go about constructing their religious worlds.

INTRODUCTION TO THE FIELD SITE

Over four hundred years ago European colonists arrived in what is now called New Mexico with the hope of finding gold and serving God. The Franciscan friars among the colonizers intended to convert the native Pueblo people to Roman Catholicism. As the Franciscans focused their efforts on the Native Americans, the European community

[15] Orsi, *Between Heaven and Earth*, 7–8.

received less attention. The European community also suffered a decrease in the number of clergy due to the wars between Mexico and Spain (1821), and Mexico and the United States (1846). It was in this context that the Hermandad (the Brotherhood) emerged throughout northern New Mexico with a number of Moradas. In Spanish, the word "Morada" has several meanings, depending on usage. The most common meaning is home, dwelling, or residence. In the phrase, "la eterna Morada," it takes on the meaning of heaven, eternal home, or the great beyond. In the phrase, "última Morada," it takes on the meaning of final resting place, as in place of burial. The way that the Penitentes use the word Morada resonates with each of these meanings. The Morada is the building, the place where they gather for meetings, prayer, penance, and meals. They even sleep there, on the floor, during Holy Week. The Morada is also a cemetery, a final resting place. Deceased Brothers and parishioners are buried on the grounds surrounding the buildings. The Morada is a place where one prays for the dead as well. Each year the Hermanos in Arroyo Seco host parishioners at the Morada for an entire evening dedicated to the dead. One year the parish bulletin described it as "A Special Night for All Souls."[16] When we hear the spiritual life stories of Larry Torres we could add another meaning; the Morada is the place where he experiences death and identifies with the dead.

The actual origins of Los Hermanos Penitentes are not known. Records indicate that people were performing acts of self-flagellation in the region in 1598. The particular village of Arroyo Seco has been home to both Pueblo people and Spanish settlers since the latter part of the seventeenth century. Its oldest known church was built in 1834 by the Hermanos. Early pictures of the first church building show a west wing on the church that was used by the Hermanos as a place for meetings and rituals. Apparently this west wing was dismantled and moved adobe by adobe to the present location after the church authorities disbanded La Fraternidad in 1854. The church of Holy Trinity in

[16] The bulletin reads, "The evening will begin with some explanations about the Feast of the Ascensión and the nature of Purgatory by Hermano ——. After that, a ritual called La Procesión de los Muertos [The Procession of the Dead] will take place. It is a special devotional procession with farolitos [paper bags with sand and candles] lit in memory of the souls of those whose names we receive. It will also include a rosary followed by a celebration of the Holy Mass right at the Morada."

Arroyo Seco is the regional center for Penitente rituals from Wednesday of Holy Week until late at night on Good Friday.

The public[17] rituals consist of praying the Stations of the Cross in the field surrounding the Morada, reenacting in the Morada, church, and church plaza scenes from the final days and death of Jesus Christ, making pilgrimages from the surrounding villages to the church plaza, processing the statues of Mary and Jesus from the various locations, and hosting a Good Friday Lenten meal in the Morada.

The Penitentes also perform private rituals during their Holy Week stay at the Morada. These rituals consist of self-flagellation and other acts of penance. Although I have limited information concerning the nature of these activities, I have obtained photographs of a series of paintings of New Mexican Penitentes done by Isaac L. Udell who addressed the medical concerns of the brothers in the earlier part of the twentieth century. These paintings are held in a private collection and are not publicly displayed because they so graphically portray the private rituals of the brotherhood.[18] These private acts of penance, performed in one of the private rooms of the Morada and in secluded places nearby, are reportedly protected by an oath of secrecy.

The Penitentes plan both the public and the private rituals and decide who performs the specific roles. In public, several of the Brothers are responsible for the speaking roles and for leading the alabados (hymns of praise). Other Brothers are responsible for carrying statues or other items in the procession. All of the rituals have silent roles, which are played primarily by Penitentes. Other men and women from the parish are invited to participate on Holy Friday by making a pilgrimage from their surrounding villages to the plaza outside the church. Although the speaking roles are performed solely by the male Penitentes, various acting roles are played by both men and women. Within the

[17] By "public" I mean that anyone is welcome to attend. When Larry Torres, a Penitente and instructor at the University of New Mexico, Taos, is in town he invites fifty to a hundred of his students to participate in the Good Friday events. By "public," I also mean that many of the rituals are performed outside, either in the village plaza or in the yard surrounding the Morada.

[18] I was able to view the Udell paintings in person. The paintings had to be pulled from storage for viewing. The curator of the collection explained to us that the paintings are in storage because of their graphic depictions of Penitente practices.

rituals themselves, there are three roles played by women. The first group is composed of the Verónicas,[19] who are young women aged thirteen and who play the role of Veronica or the Virgin Mary. The second group is composed of the Auxiliadoras (Auxiliaries), women, usually the wives or daughters of Penitentes, who participate in the prayers and processions and prepare all of the meals for the Penitentes and their guests. The last group is actually a single person who is one of only two women in northern New Mexico who are Penitentes. For over twenty years she served as the person responsible for training and guiding the Verónicas. She also participates in the processions and prayers, often helping carry the statue of the Virgin Mary. In addition to these women there are also women who participate in the pilgrimages from the surrounding villages and join the gathered assembly for the public rituals.

The indices of the major texts written about the Penitentes in northern New Mexico, rarely make any reference to Arroyo Seco. Arroyo Seco doesn't appear in Alex M. Darley's *The Passionists of the Southwest*, Alice Corbin Henderson's *Brothers of Light*, Bill Tate's *The Penitentes of the Sangre de Cristos*, Fray Angélico Chávez's *My Penitente Land*, William Wroth's *Images of Penance, Images of Mercy*, Ray John de Aragón's *Hermanos de la Luz: Brothers of the Light*, or the most recent book on the Penitentes, Michael P. Carroll's *The Penitente Brotherhood*. In addition, Arroyo Seco never made it into the WPA guides to New Mexico in the 1930s and 1940s. Marta Weigle, however, does mention Arroyo Seco in both her *Brothers of Light, Brothers of Blood* and *A Penitente Bibliography*. Each of these texts records a 1931 certificate of incorporation for Penitente Moradas of Taos County, including Arroyo Seco. In *Brothers of Light, Brothers of Blood*, Weigle briefly relates how several young girls in Arroyo Seco were selected to be the Verónicas and to assist with the enactment of the Encuentro on Good Friday morning, which I will describe in detail in the following pages.[20] In Weigle's *A Penitente Bibliography* she notes a 1954 photograph in *El Crepúsculo*, a Taos newspaper. The entry includes the explanation that

[19] According to legend, there was a woman who accompanied Jesus as he carried his cross. She wiped his face with a cloth, which retained his image. Consequently, the woman was named after the image that she bore, Veronica or true icon.

[20] Marta Weigle, *Brothers of Light, Brothers of Blood: The Penitentes of the Southwest* (Santa Fe, NM: Ancient City Press, 1976), 167–68.

the photograph included the Morada of Seco, which was reportedly sold and converted into a private home.[21] This, however, was not the case. It was the Morada of Arroyo Hondo, which was more widely known and written about, that was closed in 1954 and sold to become a home for the Clinton Bennetts. At the same time, most of its Bultos (statues) and Penitente paraphernalia were sold.

The absence of Arroyo Seco in the majority of these prominent books on the Penitentes may be one reason little attention has been paid it by other scholars. Perhaps the reports that the Morada of Arroyo Seco was sold also helped to maintain its obscurity. It is also true that until 1948, Arroyo Seco belonged to the parish in Taos. At that time, the villages that composed the parish of Taos were recon-figured. A new parish, consisting of San Antonio de Padua Church in Valdez, Nuestra Señora de Dolores in Arroyo Hondo, La Santísima Trinidad in Arroyo Seco, San Cristóbal in San Cristóbal, and Santo Niño in Las Colonias, was established by the Archdiocese of Santa Fe. After taking a census of the five churches, the archdiocese decided to establish the rectory, the residence of the priest, at La Santísima Trinidad in Arroyo Seco and to call the newly established community Holy Trinity Parish.[22] In addition, when the Morada of Arroyo Hondo was closed shortly thereafter, some of the remaining Hermanos joined the Morada of Arroyo Seco.

Even with the development of the Taos ski resorts just above Seco and the creation of Holy Trinity Parish, there continues to be a lack of documentation and exploration of the religious practices of this small village. Because the Morada of Seco continues to be one of the most active in the Brotherhood, sociologists and anthropologists do visit Seco seeking to investigate the practices of the Penitentes. Larry Torres, the archivist for the Seco Morada and a member of the Penitentes for over forty years, told me during the initial stages of my inquiry that academics come around each year hoping to get some glimpse of the inner life of the Penitentes in this mountain village. In response to their inquiries, Larry usually tells them that they are welcome to par-ticipate in the public rituals of the parish and Brotherhood, as long as

[21] Marta Weigle, *A Penitente Bibliography* (Albuquerque, NM: University of New Mexico Press, 1976), 148.

[22] Rev. Vincent P. Chávez, interview by author, tape recording, Santa Fe, NM, December 7, 2003.

they do not attempt to record or photograph any event. They are welcome to whatever they can gather from participating in those events, Torres tells them. He denies their requests for interviews or any other documentation.

RESEARCH METHODS

I chose the village of Arroyo Seco for three reasons. First of all, I already had an entree into this community through my seminary classmate, who was a former pastor, and I had begun to develop a relationship with the people during my first visit in 1995. The second reason was that the Morada in Arroyo Seco was one of the largest and most active Moradas in New Mexico. Third, the Morada in Arroyo Seco was one of only two Moradas in New Mexico that had a female Penitenta.

I had two goals as an ethnographer in this project. My first goal was to document as much as possible the activities of the Brotherhood in Arroyo Seco during the years of my research (1999–2003). This became particularly important to me once I realized that even though there have been a significant number of books published about the Penitentes in northern New Mexico and southern Colorado, there has been little mention of Arroyo Seco. The second goal of my research was to get a clearer understanding of what these Roman Catholics are doing and what these practices mean to them, in light of their particular history and context.

For this project I used a variety of research methods and resources: participant observation; interviewing; collecting spiritual life stories; analyzing video recordings, paintings, historical artifacts, and buildings; reviewing local newspaper columns, local radio programs, locally published books, and church bulletins; and library research. During the years of my research, I made five trips to Arroyo Seco in order to participate in different events that are celebrated throughout the year. Three of those visits (1999, 2001, 2002) were organized around participating in the Holy Week services. The other two visits were in September and December of 2002. In addition to these five encounters, I visited Seco once before I had chosen it as a research site. I participated in the Holy Week services in the spring of 1995. That was my first encounter with the Penitentes. Since there can be more than one activity happening at the same time during Holy Week, successive visits allowed me to participate in different aspects of the same events. For example, the first year I was accompanying the pastor and his participation in the services. The following visit I accompanied the Penitentes. Another visit allowed me to spend time in the kitchens where some of the women were preparing meals.

In addition to attending the Holy Week services, I also participated in one of the parish feast days, Nuestra Señora de los Dolores (Our Lady of Sorrows), which is celebrated on or near September 15 of each year. A description of this event can be found in appendix 1. During a December visit to Seco I participated in Las Posadas, which commemorates the story of Mary and Joseph searching for a place to stay the night. A description of this event can be found in appendix 2. I have included them because they were among the ritual events that formed the larger, yearly cycle of events in Holy Trinity Parish during the years of my research. They were also part of the yearly cycle of Penitente events.[23] In both instances they included the participation of the Penitentes from the Morada in Arroyo Seco. In other villages this may not have been the case. Each Morada has its own relationship with the local church. In addition to attending the events noted above, I also attended the feast day celebration in Taos for Our Lady of Guadalupe, a traditional pole climbing ritual at Picuris Pueblo, and Mass on a regular basis in Seco.

Doing ethnographic research among people who perform secret practices presents ethical and practical challenges for the researcher. Access can be severely restricted. Having access does not automatically mean that people will be willing to talk or be willing to have their ideas published. When access is obtained, ethical issues emerge quickly. A researcher can upset or harm a practitioner by asking questions that will require the interviewee to break their codes of secrecy. The original research protocol for this project included interviewing a sampling of people who participate in the Penitente rituals throughout the year: the Penitentes, the Verónicas, the Auxiliadoras, the parish priests, the parishioners, and visitors, both local and from outside the community. Practical limitations, however, prevented consulting such

---

[23] In fact, there are a number of events that made up the repertoire of events in Arroyo Seco. A complete ethnographic study of the Penitentes in Arroyo Seco would need to take a closer look at the many activities that have been included in their yearly cycle and at the way in which that repertoire has shifted over the years. In addition, each participant would also have his or her own personal repertoire of activities, e.g., private devotions that would intersect with that of the community.

a wide sample. The limitations stemmed from the fact that the activities of the Hermanos are surrounded by rules of secrecy, which they have been asked to keep by the Archdiocese of Santa Fe. Permission for the Hermanos to participate in such research projects can be approved by the governing body of the Hermandad, the Mesa Directiva. I was not able to get explicit permission to officially interview members of the Penitente Brotherhood. My requests for permission were met not with denial but with silence. Rather than ask the members and the other participants to compromise their relationship with the Mesa, with the possibility of jeopardizing the entire research project, I decided not to do taped interviews with members of the Hermandad or the Auxiliadoras and Verónicas. While trying to obtain permission from the Mesa, I also learned through the relatives of the one female Penitenta in Seco that she wasn't willing, and never has been, to talk about her experiences as a member. It's public knowledge that she participates in the sacred dramas that the Penitentes perform during Holy Week, but I was told by one Hermano that because she was a woman, she had to perform her acts of penance in her home.

At the same time that I was realizing the limits of my access to the community, I also believed that a deeper look at the experiences of one member could be just as beneficial, if not more so. I decided to approach Hermano Larry Torres, who is a catechist and the archivist for the Morada in Seco, to participate in my research project. Larry has been a member for over forty years and plays a key role in the organizing and performance of the Brotherhood's public activities. He is also one of the few Penitentes who speaks and writes regularly about the history of their activities in northern New Mexico. Through the lens of his spiritual life stories, Larry doesn't disclose anything new about the practices of the Hermandad. He doesn't violate any of their rules. He does, however, provide us with an account of his experiences of being an Hermano. This is something new.[24]

The activities of the La Fraternidad Piadosa de Nuestro Padre Jesús Nazareno and the experiences of the various participants are worthy of a complete ethnographic study. The rich juxtaposition of the Penitente practices with official Roman Catholic liturgies is an important site of primary theology. Due to the practical limitations involved, I had to limit the scope of my research. The implications of the limita-

[24] Larry gave permission for his name to be used both in the dissertation and this book.

tions of this project will be taken up in chapters 3 and 4. Besides the issues I have outlined here, we'll also look at how changes in my relationship with the Roman Catholic Church affected my role as researcher in the field.

CHAPTER REVIEW

There are two conversations happening within the pages of this book. The first and the wider one is about the role of ethnographic research within theology and theological studies. There are a number of ways to have that conversation. I chose to engage it by experimenting with the practice of doing ethnographic research, which takes us to the second conversation. That is about the particular ritual behaviors of the Penitente Brotherhood in the northern New Mexican village of Arroyo Seco. The research that I did was not an exhaustive ethnographic study, but it was an exploration of their practices sufficient enough to illustrate how imperative it is for theologians and pastoral ministers to engage Christians about their lived experience. At the same time, the results of this research make a contribution to the body of literature available about the Penitente Brotherhood.

In this introduction we have raised the question concerning what we theologians can learn from engaging Christians more explicitly about their lives. We have situated the question and its importance in the context of Aidan Kavanagh's proposal to restore Christian worship to its primary place within theological studies, and consequently, restore Christian worshipers to their roles as primary theologians. If Christian worshipers are primary theologians, we should be taking their experiences and how they understand them more seriously. I have chosen to explore this claim by doing ethnographic research with the Penitente Brotherhood in Arroyo Seco, New Mexico.

Chapter 1 provides the reader with the historical context of the Penitente Brotherhood in northern New Mexico and Arroyo Seco in particular. The chapter traces what is known at this point about the development of the Hermandad, without attempting to solve the questions about its origins. Chapter 1 also introduces the reader to the key persons in the Brotherhood's history in New Mexico and to a longstanding member of the Morada in Arroyo Seco, Larry Torres.

Chapter 2 takes us directly into the most active week within the Penitente yearly calendar of events: Holy Week. The first part of this chapter documents the various activities of the Penitentes during Holy Week and how those events interconnect with the other Holy Week services that are part of the official rites sponsored by the church. The centerpiece of the chapter is a thick description of El Encuentro (The Encounter), which is the reenactment of Mary and Jesus encountering each other as Jesus carries his cross. In this account, we get a glimpse of the complexities of the Penitente practices and of the experiences of the participants. Throughout this chapter, we'll see Larry Torres emerge as a central figure in the performance of these practices and in the life of this community.

Chapter 3 focuses on the experiences of Larry Torres as a Penitente. In this chapter I include a significant portion of the transcript from the spiritual life stories that we recorded, along with my commentary. This chapter also describes how developments within my own life impacted and interacted with the research process. Far from being incidental, the particular dynamics of the interactions between Larry and me shaped my conception of ethnographic research as a theological act.

In chapter 4 we return to the two conversations proposed in this introduction: the contribution that ethnographic research can make to theological studies and what the Hermanos Penitentes in Arroyo Seco do and how they interpret those practices within their context. We'll begin with the latter conversation because it will provide us with a lively illustration of how ethnographic research can be a powerful way to reflect with other Christians and to engage them in dialogue about their spiritual practices, their everyday lives, and the ways in which they interpret those experiences. In the end, we'll see that ethnographic research can go beyond gathering data and learning to see others more clearly. Ethnographic research can also be an act of primary theology. That is, it can also be the faith of the church in action.

Four appendixes follow chapter 4. Appendix 1 provides a description of the Vespers service for the parish feast day of Nuestra Señora de los Dolores (Our Lady of Sorrows). I have included it here because it provides the reader with additional information about the ritual activities of the Arroyo Seco Morada. This feast day celebration is another example of how the Penitentes play a prominent role in the life of the community. This particular account also illustrates Larry's role within the community, including his relationship with the pastor and the parish community. The second appendix presents an account of another celebration from the calendar of events of the Arroyo Seco community: Las Posadas. The Penitentes as a group are not central in the festivities, but the way this celebration is executed in Arroyo Seco adds to our understanding of the particularities of the larger community. In this description of the first night of Las Posadas we also see yet another view of Larry's role within the community. The third appendix offers the reader a much fuller transcription of Larry's spiritual life stories. Offered here without additional comment, the transcription gives a direct account of Larry's voice and his own self-conscious leadership. Appendix 4 provides two illustrations from Larry's picture book for children about the bogey creatures of the Southwest. I also include his descriptions of the illustrations. In offering all four of these appendixes, I intend to help bring the Penitente Brotherhood and their practices into fuller focus for the reader.

Chapter 1

Historical Background

THE PAPAL MEDALLION

In December 2002 Larry Torres handed me a copy of the next article to appear in his weekly column, Cruising the Camino Real, published in *The Taos News*. "Maybe It's Time to Make Peace with the Pope" was at the top of the first page.[1] The newspaper's online description of his column notes that, "It allows Torres the opportunity to address the multiple historical events, beliefs, traditions and family records that reveal what northern New Mexico has become across the centuries through the eyes of its Hispanic population." In this particular install-ment, Torres tells the story of how the people of Holy Trinity Parish in Arroyo Seco, New Mexico, found buried, face down, in the sanctu-ary's mud floor a gold-plated copper medallion of Pope Pius IX. The medallion was retrieved in 1996 during a restoration of the adobe La Santísima Trinidad Church. The church was built in 1834, but had been nearly abandoned since 1961, when another, larger Holy Trinity Church was built across the plaza.

According to Torres, the local church has carried resentment toward Pius IX. Finding the medallion opened up "a deep wound in the history of the Catholic Church in northern New Mexico." In his column, Torres continues by recounting how Pius IX was the pope who told Archbishop Jean Baptiste Lamy, the first bishop of Santa Fe, to disband the Penitente Brotherhood. Soon after Archbishop Lamy had visited Rome in 1854, he visited Padre Antonio José Martínez, who was both the pastor of Taos and the spiritual head of the Penitente Brotherhood. Lamy relayed to Martínez the pope's directive to disband the Penitente Brotherhood and all similar organizations. As pastor of Taos at that time, Martínez was also the pastor of Arroyo Seco, where records indicate that the present Morada of the Penitente Brotherhood of Seco dates from 1870.

---

[1] Larry T. Torres, "Maybe It's Time to Make Peace with the Pope," Cruising the Camino Real, *The Taos News*, December 26, 2002.

Upon analyzing a Gene Kloss sketch of the original La Santísima Trinidad Church, Torres conjectures that the original west transept of the 1834 church was the meeting room of the Penitentes until Pius IX ordered their disbandment. Torres suggested that sometime before 1870 the Penitentes moved their Morada adobe by adobe across the road to their present location. And in using the papal souvenir to make a statement of protest, they buried the blessed article face down in the mud floor of the church.

Since finding the medallion in 1996, Torres has been reconsidering "the great disfavor that the pope showed to the Penitentes of New Mexico." Moved by reports that Pius IX used to walk barefoot across Rome at night to rest upon the relics of Jesus' crib, Torres suggests that Pius IX's decision to disband the Penitente Brotherhood was "due more to inexperience than to malice. . . . Any man who can humble himself before a baby's crib is certainly a man who might have been different if he had only been better informed."[2] After carrying resentment against Pius IX since the 1850s, Torres thinks that perhaps it is time for the Brotherhood and Holy Trinity Parish to make peace with this pope.

This series of interconnecting and overlapping stories introduces the reader to some of the key figures in the history of Holy Trinity Parish of Arroyo Seco. At the same time the narrative reveals many of the rich complexities of this small, predominantly Roman Catholic village of northern New Mexico, which will allow us to explore the contributions of ethnographic research to theological and liturgical studies. Larry Torres's column of December 26, 2002, was not simply a history lesson for Taoseños. He was offering absolution to a pope from the 1850s who had made decisions affecting the life of his village. Torres's column was performatory.

After all these years, what precipitated such reconciliation between the Catholic Church in northern New Mexico and Pope Pius IX? Pius IX was beatified on September 3, 2000, and in the research process before his beatification, it was reportedly discovered that he had a practice of secretly slipping out of the Vatican at night in order to rest upon pieces of Jesus' baby crib, now housed in the Basilica of St. Mary Major in Rome. Torres writes that this discovery moved him to offer forgiveness to Pius IX. Let's look at Torres's words of absolution again: "Any man who can humble himself before a baby's crib is certainly a man who might have been different if he had only been better informed." Despite

---

[2] Ibid.

the pope's devotion and his beatification, Torres maintains that Pius IX remains in the wrong about his decision to disband the Hermandad. Torres could interpret the story differently. He could conclude that since the pope had such humility and was beatified, he must have been right to disband the Penitentes. But Torres doesn't. Instead he concludes that the pope must have had insufficient information about the practices of the Brotherhood when he chose to disband them.

Recent discoveries about the devotional life of Pius IX weren't the only factors that led Torres to pronounce his absolution. The finding of the gold-plated medallion in the mud floor of the old church also played an important role in this process. In his column, Torres makes a point that I heard other members of the renovation crew make: the medallion was found face down in the mud. While this place-ment of the medallion served to preserve it in excellent condition, the *interpretation* of this placement is what stands out. Torres and the renovation crew take the face-down position of the medallion as an act of resistance on the part of their ancestors. Thought to be a papal souvenir, a gift blessed by Pius IX and given to his visitors, Torres and the pastor responsible for the renovation, Rev. Vincent Chávez, believe that Lamy might have brought the medallion to Seco when he met with Padre Martínez of Taos to deliver the pope's instruction to disband the Penitentes. Signifying their refusal of the pope's mandate to disband, the Penitentes buried the medallion in the ground under-neath the church. By burying the papal souvenir in the ground, the Brothers were following the longstanding Roman Catholic custom of burying sacred items, rather than throwing them away.

While the stories about the devotional life of Pius IX changed Torres's perception of the pope, the medallion and its placement changed the way Torres and other parishioners of Seco perceived them-selves. Finding the image of Pius IX in this way, in the mud, legitimized the "deep wound in the history of the Catholic Church in northern New Mexico." After nearly one hundred and fifty years of living with the pope's decision to disband the Penitentes and fifty years since the 1947 reconciliation between the Penitentes and the archbishop of Santa Fe, the discovery of the medallion makes the wound tangible. Not only that, the placement of the medallion tells Torres and his pastor that their ancestors did not succumb to the pope's demands. The combina-tion of the discovery of the medallion and the stories of Pius IX's devo-tions gave Torres the opportunity to offer the pope absolution for his actions without either side being humiliated.

Nestled between Carson National Forest and Taos Pueblo lands, Arroyo Seco is a small farming and ranching village at the foot of the Sangre de Cristo Mountain Range, just eight miles northeast of Taos. Before the Taos Ski Valley opened in 1955,[3] few people outside of New Mexico would have known about "Seco," as the locals call it. Since then, thousands of skiers drive through Seco each winter when they want to ski on the slopes of the Taos Ski Valley. Nonetheless, well-known politicians, actors, actresses, and businesspeople continue to seek out Seco as a refuge from the world and as a place to live in privacy. Despite its popularity for skiing in the winter and river rafting in the spring, Seco remains an isolated village of the United States, just as it was an isolated village of Mexico and Spain in previous times.

Although little information is presently available, local historians believe that members of the Anasazi people (the ancestral Pueblo people), who were responsible for building Pueblo Bonito at Chaco Canyon, dwelt in the Seco-Taos area centuries before the region was explored by Francisco Vásquez de Coronado and claimed as a possession of Spain in 1540.[4] By the time that Capitan Hernando Alvarado of Coronado's exploration team arrived in the area, the Taos Pueblo had already been built by the Tiwa-speaking Pueblo people.[5] The Taos area, however, remained relatively unsettled by Spanish explorers until Don Juan de Oñate officially established settlements in the region in 1598.

Between 1598, when Oñate firmly established settlements in northern New Mexico for the kingdom of Spain, and 1680, when the Pueblo Revolt led by Popé drove the Spanish missionaries and colonizers to retreat to El Paso del Norte (El Paso), the Spanish village of Taos was

---

[3] James C. Bull, *Out of Time: Arroyo Seco: An Historic Look at a 250 Year Old Northern New Mexico Village* (Taos, NM: Wolf Publishing Works, 1998), 44.

[4] Bull calls the Anasazi the First People of Arroyo Seco and suggests that wandering members from Chaco Canyon began to settle there in pit houses along the banks of the river. See Bull, *Out of Time*, 14.

[5] Coronado's expedition into New Mexico was based on reports from Franciscan Friar Marcos de Niza, who with his Moorish slave Estévanico, previously explored the area in 1539. Estévanico was killed during the expedition, but de Niza returned to Viceroy Antonio de Mendoza in Mexico with reports of potential wealth in the northern Indian villages. For a concise summary of the history of New Mexico see Myra Ellen Jenkins and Albert H. Schroeder, *A Brief History of New Mexico* (Albuquerque: University of New Mexico Press, 1974).

established, probably around 1615. During that same period a Spanish land grant of nearly sixty thousand acres was given to Diego Lucero de Godoy.[6] The grant included the area of present-day Arroyo Seco. After the revolt of 1680, Godoy never returned to his lands in the Arroyo Seco region.

In 1692, the king of Spain reconquered the territory of New Mexico through the new leadership of Governor Don Diego de Vargas Zapata Luján Ponce de León y Contreras, better known as de Vargas. The process of rebuilding and refounding the Spanish settlements of New Mexico began in 1693 by de Vargas, seventy families, one hundred soldiers, and seventeen Franciscans. Despite de Vargas's success at quickly defeating a second Pueblo revolt in 1696, a number of Franciscans were killed. The successful "reconquest" of New Mexico by de Vargas and his forces was attributed, in part, to a small wooden statue of Our Lady of the Assumption which they believed was originally brought to New Mexico in 1624 and was rescued during the Pueblo revolt. In gratitude for her assistance, the statue was renamed La Conquistadora.[7]

The time between de Vargas's resettlement of New Mexico and Mexico's independence from Spain in 1821 was marked by ongoing conflicts among the various peoples inhabiting the region: the Spanish authorities, the Pueblo Indian peoples, the Nomadic Indian peoples, the Franciscan friars, and the diocesan bishops. While Spanish authorities and the Pueblo Indians had uneasy relationships, they were often unified in their defense against attacks from nomadic or migrating Apaches, Navajos, Utes, and Commanches. In the meantime, as the shrinking Franciscan community sought to expand their missionary activities into new territories in the West, the bishop of Durango, Mexico, sought to exercise spiritual authority in what was considered his jurisdiction. As the Franciscan population died off or migrated into new territory, diocesan priests were assigned to provide spiritual leadership.[8]

---

[6] Bull, *Out of Time*, 20.

[7] For a ritual analysis of the celebration of La Conquistadora in Santa Fe, see Ronald L. Grimes, *Symbol and Conquest: Public Ritual and Drama in Santa Fe* (Albuquerque: University of New Mexico Press, 1992).

[8] Diocesan priests, often referred to as "secular priests," differ in several ways from priests like the Franciscans, who are members of a religious community. Diocesan priests do not take vows of poverty, they are not required

The Taos area, which actually included much of northern New Mexico from Ranchos de Taos (just south of present day Taos) up into present-day southern Colorado, underwent tremendous change during the eighteenth century. After killing the Commanche leader Cuerno Verde, Juan Bautista de Anza established a treaty with the Commanches in 1786. Attacks by other nomadic peoples remained a threat, but the treaty of 1786 allowed for the population of Ranchos de Taos to expand northward up the Sangre de Cristo Mountains.

Begun during the Spanish rule of New Mexico, and honored under Mexican rule, a system of bestowing grants of governmental lands to either heads of individual Spanish families or to entire communities was enacted. In Arroyo Seco, the land that was abandoned by Diego Lucero de Godoy after the Pueblo Revolt of 1680 was regranted to Don Antonio Martínez in 1716. Between one and two miles northeast of the present-day plaza of Arroyo Seco, are the ruins of a torreón (tower) positioned just high enough in the mountains to give visual access to the region. Recent studies by local archeologist Jeffrey L. Boyer, which dates the original construction of the torreón at 1745, supports local claims that the original center of Arroyo Seco was upstream before it eventually was relocated to its present location surrounding La Santísima Trinidad Church.[9]

Boyer believes that the torreón provided both a lookout for potential raids from Apaches and Commanches and a place of protection, should one be too far from home during an attack. Boyer also states that before the treaty with the Commanches the area of Arroyo Seco was populated by a few ranchers and farmers, scattered across the valley. After the treaty, however, Spanish settlers from Ranchos de Taos began to move northward into the Taos valley.

In addition, in 1821, when Mexico achieved its independence from Spain, the new leadership of the Republic of Mexico decided to permit foreign traders to enter into its territory and to do business. Traders from the United States began crossing Raton Pass and entering the newly established province of New Mexico, creating what quickly became the Santa Fe Trail. William Becknell, the first trader to seize the opportunity of new trade prospects, followed the Cimarron route to

---

to live in community with other priests, and their immediate superior is the bishop or archbishop of the diocese. Typically, the ministry of the diocesan or secular priest is the local parish community.

[9] Jeffrey L. Boyer, phone interview by author, April 2, 2003.

Santa Fe. An offshoot of the trail brought traders, goods, and trappers to Taos. Consequently, the village experienced a moderate increase in economic activity and growth. The Taos Trade Fairs, where produce, dried goods, and handmade items had been traded for decades, grew to their height in the late 1700s, as the fairs expanded to include French and American trappers and traders and their wares.

Taos, however, wasn't directly on the Santa Fe Trail. When train travel arrived in New Mexico in the late nineteenth century it was bypassed again. The Sangre de Cristo Mountains made access to Taos Valley difficult. For this reason, it did not prosper to the extent that Santa Fe did. But, as traffic and commerce along the Santa Fe Trail increased and raids from Commanches and Apaches decreased, the number of settlements in New Mexico grew, including the area of Taos and Arroyo Seco.

Receiving new settlers from both the south and the north, Arroyo Seco saw a significant growth in population in the late 1700s and early 1800s. In 1745 the same tract of land that had been granted to Antonio Martínez was granted to Antonio Martín. Upon his death a dispute arose among his heirs. A settlement in 1826 awarded the land above the arroyo to the Sanches family. This property was subdivided among the members of the family, with a portion of it used for the Arroyo Seco plaza. The remaining land, south of the arroyo, was awarded to the Martín family, who sold it to the Taos Pueblo.

Also in 1826, permission from the Diocese of Durango, Mexico, was given for the construction of a church in the plaza of Arroyo Seco.[10] In that same year, Padre Antonio José Martínez became the pastor of Taos, which included not only Taos, but also the outlying areas, including Arroyo Seco. Completed in 1834, La Santísima Trinidad Church was built, reportedly, by the Hermanos of Seco. San Antonio de Padua church in Valdez, which also belonged to the Taos parish at that period and presently is one of the other churches in Holy Trinity Parish, was completed in 1826, and was consecrated in 1842. Although

[10] According to the archives of the Archdiocese of Durango, Bishop Juan Francisco Castañiza Larrea y Gonzalez de Agüero was the ordinary from 1816–1825. Bishop José Antonio Laureano de Zubiría y Escalante wasn't appointed until 1831, which would suggest that although approval was given to build a church in Arroyo Seco (under the auspices of the parish of Taos), there was limited oversight of the activities of these small village communities. Zubiría served as the ordinary of Durango until his death in 1863.

there is no extant evidence for the consecration of the church in Seco, former pastor Rev. Vincent Chávez believes that La Santísima Trinidad was consecrated by Zubiría during the same trip in which the church in Valdez was consecrated.

At the same time that the Hermanos were building the church in Arroyo Seco, their pastor, Padre Martínez was writing to Bishop Zubiría about the presence of La Hermandad de la Sangre de Cristo (the Brotherhood of the Blood of Christ) in his parish. In February 1833, Martínez wrote,

> In the time that I have had in my charge the spiritual administration of this parish [San Gerónimo de Taos], there has been a congregation of men in a Brotherhood of the Blood of Christ, who make exercises of penance during the Lenten seasons principally on Fridays, all of Holy Week, Fridays from this time until Pentecost, and other days of such significance in the year. These exercises consist of dragging wooden crosses, whipping themselves with scourges, that they have for the purpose, piercing their backs with sharp stones or flints until the blood flows; and other rigorous means such as the following: They walk barefoot, even over the snows, and [illegible]; naked, with only certain coverings over their private parts, or in white short trousers, and neckerchiefs over their faces in order not to be recognized, and yet to be able to see. In the said days of Lent and all those of Holy Week, they do this everywhere by day, but in the processions of Holy Week, they have the custom of marching in front of the images in the manner described, so that they cause a great spectacle to the bystanders. They say that thus it has been granted to them from time immemorial.

> For the present: I have suspended their public activity and have permitted them only to do it at night and during the day in solitary places, because it makes me very uneasy, the manner in which they have done it until now, and more so since their number has increased. Also it has scattered discord among them and other consequences that cause scandal. So in the meantime I am consulting your Lordship as to what I should prescribe for them in this case: whether they should continue, be modified or simply just cease.[11]

---

[11] William Wroth, *Images of Penance, Images of Mercy: Southwestern Santos in the Late Nineteenth Century* (Norman: University of Oklahoma Press, 1991), 40. For the Spanish text of Martínez's letter, Zubiría's response, and a report from Zubiría's visit in April 1833, see 172–73. (Wroth translates the first paragraph on page 40 of his text. I have translated the second paragraph from the

Although we know that the Hermanos were active in Seco during the time that Martínez was pastor, there is no evidence that he was writing to Zubiría about the Hermanos of Seco. The territory of the Taos parish was expansive and its mission churches were many. Having become their pastor in 1826, however, we can be confident that Martínez would have been familiar with the Hermanos of Seco and their activities there.

In his response to Martínez, Bishop Zubiría affirmed the pastor's decision to limit the Hermanos' penitential activities. Both the bishop and the pastor focused on the fact that the acts were done publicly and that they were excessive. According to Zubiría, such excessiveness is harmful to both the body and the soul.[12] In April 1833, he wrote, "in regard to which the best way to please Him is to listen to and docilely obey the voice of their pastors, being content for now with doing penances in the privacy of the church, always with moderation."[13] A few months later Zubiría visited New Mexico and published a special letter in which he reiterated his position that although the Hermandad de Penitentes had existed for some time and that performing private acts of penance in moderation could be spiritually beneficial, he prohibited all organized, public, penitential activities of the Brotherhood.[14] In fact, Zubiría went even further in this letter. He prohibited the construction of any building or place where the Brothers could gather for activities or where they could store the large wood crosses that they used for penance. At the end of his pastoral visitation to New Mexico in October 1833, Zubiría published a pastoral letter in which he stated once again his concern with "esas hermandades de penitencia ó más bien de carnicería,"[15] these brotherhoods of penance or better, of butchery.

Despite Zubiría's pronouncements in 1833, he found the Hermandad continuing their practices of public penance in 1845, when he returned for a second pastoral visit. In response, the bishop had his letter of 1833 read again in the parishes of New Mexico. There is no record of Zubiría addressing the subject again when he returned for his third

---

Spanish on pages 172–73.) The original letters are held by the archives of the Diocese of Durango.

[12] Ibid.

[13] Ibid., 51.

[14] Marta Weigle, *Brothers of Light: Brothers of Blood: The Penitentes of the Southwest* (Santa Fe, NM: Ancient City Press, 1976), 195–96.

[15] Ibid., 196.

(and final) pastoral visit to New Mexico in 1850. By that time New Mexico had become a possession of the United States, and Zubiría was more concerned with the ways in which the Roman Catholic faith of these communities could be jeopardized by the invasion of nonbelievers.

While Zubiría was making his third pastoral visitation in New Mexico, the pope in Rome, at the request of the Provincial Council of Baltimore, was creating a new vicariate for the United States' newly acquired territory of New Mexico.[16] Jean Baptiste Lamy, who was born in France but working in Covington, Kentucky, was named the new vicar. Arriving in August of 1851, Lamy took up his role of spiritual leader of the Vicariate Apostolic of New Mexico. Shortly thereafter, perhaps as early as 1853, Lamy began publishing sets of rules for the Brotherhood of Penance.[17] Concerning Lamy's rules of 1856, Marta Weigle writes, "These rules have three main thrusts: regulation of the Confraternity by the priests and prelate, specifications of the responsibilities of the Hermano Mayor and other officers of the Brotherhood, and definition of membership procedures, including the rights and duties of the full-fledged Brothers."[18] In 1857 Lamy reaffirmed his previously published rules and promulgated five more rules for the Penitentes, which primarily addressed issues of membership.

Among the rules of 1856 and 1857, several of them need to be highlighted here. In rules 9 and 10 of 1856, Lamy situated the Hermanos within the hierarchy of the Roman church by making it clear that the members of the Hermandad were to be obedient to the bishop of the diocese, at that moment Lamy, and to the pastor of the parish in which their particular Morada was located. This obedience was to be performed without any complaining and with the awareness that the

[16] Thomas J. Steele, ed. and trans., *Archbishop Lamy: In His Own Words* (Albuquerque, NM: LPD Press, 2000), 9–10.

[17] Weigle reports that the earliest set of rules, dated February 17, 1853, which Chávez noted were in the archives of the Archdiocese of Santa Fe, are no longer there. See Alex M. Darley, *The Passionists of the Southwest or the Holy Brotherhood: A Revelation of the "Penitentes"* (1893; repr., Glorieta, NM: Rio Grande Press, 1968) for a copy of "The Constitution," dated February 17, 1860, which Weigle believes resembles closely the 1853 document. For the 1856 edition of Lamy's rules and the five additional rules that he published in 1857, see Weigle, *Brothers of Light*, 201–6.

[18] Weigle, *Brothers of Light*, 54.

bishop enjoyed the freedom to move their pastor to another parish at any time. Just as the Brothers were to be accountable and obedient to their pastor, rule 10 stated, their pastor was to be accountable and obedient to the bishop.

Rule 3 of 1856, as it is recorded by Weigle, states:

> All brothers must keep secret all matters that may be transacted at the meetings to be had and the President [Hermano Mayor] shall himself or through another notify the parish Priest in order that he may attend and be present at all meetings, if he so desires. If any one of the brothers should break the secrets he shall be severely reprimanded according to the disposition of the President (Hermano Mayor) and councellors and if he after being admonished should insist, he shall be expelled from the brotherhood.[19]

Unlike Zubiría, who mandated that the Hermanos do their acts of penance in the *privacy* of the church or their homes, Lamy placed all the proceedings of the Brotherhood under the rule of *secrecy*. Apart from the membership, only their priests and their bishop were permitted to know the details of their activities. In the rules that Lamy added in 1857, he stated that their acts of penance, "must be done, as hidden as possible, without giving scandal, to the rest of the faithful according to the spirit of the Church and without doing it with vain-glory."[20]

Concerning the issue of membership, Lamy declared in rules 4 and 5 of 1856 and rule 3 of 1857 that the Hermano Mayor (the head Penitente of the Morada) was to screen candidates for membership closely. Recent criminals or those guilty of "vices" were not to be welcomed into the Brotherhood. More particularly, "murderers, adulterers and thieves and other men, who on account of their former habits"[21] were also prohibited from membership.

Whatever Lamy's opinion of these Brotherhoods of Penance, he took a very different position with them than did his predecessor Zubiría. Instead of condemning them as brotherhoods of butchery, he issued rules stating clearly that the members of the brotherhoods must be

---

[19] Ibid., 201–2. While I'm not aware of anyone being expelled from the Brotherhood on account of breaking the rule of secrecy (rule 3), I am aware of a case in 2004, in which an Hermano was expelled for breaking rule 9, the rule demanding respect and obedience to the archbishop and the Mesa Directiva.

[20] Ibid., 205.

[21] Ibid.

obedient to him (rule 9), and must maintain secrecy concerning all the practices and activities of the Brotherhood. While admitting the importance of performing moderate acts of penance in private, Zubiría had sought to disband the Brotherhood as a penitential organization by prohibiting them from assembling publicly and by forbidding local churches from offering them space to meet or even to store their implements of penance. As noted above, Zubiría's approach was not successful.

Lamy, instead, inserted the Brotherhood into the hierarchical structure of the church, which allowed them to continue within a context of strict accountability to and close scrutiny by their pastors and the bishop. Having situated the Hermandad within the larger institution in this way he began imposing restrictions on its membership.[22]

In 1875, the Diocese of Santa Fe was elevated to an archdiocese. In July 1885, Lamy retired and Jean Baptiste Salpointe was named the new archbishop of Santa Fe. Salpointe arrived at his position of archbishop with over twenty-five years of experience working in the churches of the Southwest, first in Santa Fe and Mora, New Mexico, and later in Tucson, Arizona. Within two months of becoming the new spiritual leader of the Archdiocese of Santa Fe, Salpointe issued rules concerning the Hermandad and additional rules pertaining to all Catholic associations that already existed within the archdiocese or that would be newly established. Following Pope Leo XIII's interest to establish and foster Catholic lay associations that would be faithful to the church, Salpointe sought to revive the Third Order of St. Francis, originally called the Order of Penance.[23] Hoping both to follow the di-

[22] Weigle notes that in the archives of the Archdiocese of Santa Fe there is also a letter from Martínez to Lamy, dated November 27, 1856, in which the pastor of Taos recalls that Lamy had previously related the Holy Father's order to disband such fraternities as the Penitentes. This is entirely possible, since Pius IX (1846–1878) published directives in 1846, 1849, and 1854 that all secret societies should be disbanded, and Lamy traveled to Rome in early 1854. Unfortunately, there is no textual evidence of Lamy's remarks about such extinguishing of the fraternity beyond the letter from Padre Martínez.

[23] The Third Order of St. Francis first began as a way for lay Roman Catholics to follow a life of penance and charity while continuing to honor their social and family commitments. Today they are known as Tertiaries or the Secular Franciscan Order. See Fray Angélico Chávez, *My Penitente Land: Reflections on Spanish New Mexico* (Santa Fe, NM: Museum of Santa Fe Press, 1974), 107–9.

rectives of the pope and to build on the history of Franciscan presence in New Mexico, Salpointe encouraged Roman Catholics to pursue the practice of penance and obedience by joining the Third Order.

In particular, in 1886 Salpointe encouraged the leaders of the Hermandad de Nuestro Padre Jesús to distribute the rules of the Third Order so that they could see for themselves that the penitential practices of the Hermandad came directly from St. Francis's Order of Penance.[24] Salpointe, however, went even further. He asserted that the Brothers "must *return* to her [the Third Order of St. Francis], if they wish to obtain the Indulgences which have been granted to the Order by the Supreme Pontiff."[25] Salpointe concluded his statement, which was published in the diocesan Catholic newspaper *La Revista Católica*, by stating that he was dispensing them from the penitential practices of the Brotherhood that were not included in the practices of the Third Order and, therefore, prohibiting the flagellation and the dragging of wooden crosses that they had been practicing heretofore in public. In 1889 Salpointe repeated his call for the Brothers to dissolve the Hermandad and to become members of the Franciscan Third Order. Despite Salpointe's insistence that the Hermandad *return* not only to its Franciscan roots, but also to its official position within the hierarchical structure of the Roman Catholic Church, the Brothers continued to perform their penitential practices and refused to disband.

Recent scholarship on the history of the Penitente Brotherhood in New Mexico claims that Salpointe's decision to create a liaison between the Third Order of St. Francis and the Penitentes was an act of historical construction. Alberto López Pulido argues that Salpointe created the link between the two organizations as a way to gain control over the Brotherhood in the hopes that this would silence its members.[26] Supporting this claim is Salpointe's 1886 letter to the Brotherhood in which he tells pastors to refrain from celebrating Mass in the Morada and to withhold the sacraments from members of the Brotherhood if they refused to submit to the new Third Order rules.[27]

[24] For the entire text of Salpointe's 1886 comments on the Third Order of St. Francis and the Hermandad, see Weigle, *Brothers of Light*, 207–8.

[25] Ibid. Translation and emphasis mine.

[26] Alberto López Pulido, *The Sacred World of the Penitentes* (Washington, DC: Smithsonian Institution Press, 2000), 48–51.

[27] Weigle, *Brothers of Light*, 207–8. Also, for the most recent review of the different theories about the origins of the Brotherhood, including the possibility

From the time of his installation as Archbishop of Santa Fe in 1885 until he stepped down in 1894, Salpointe, like his predecessor Lamy, sought to bring the Hermandad under the authority of the priests, bishops, and the pope. The Brothers, however, although willing to abide by the rules that Salpointe had originally published in 1885, resisted the archbishop's actions to subsume the Hermandad into the Third Order of St. Francis.[28] Weigle notes that his lack of influence over the Brothers might have been what provoked Salpointe to write in 1892, "not only do we not progress, but we are perceptibly retrogressing year by year, with the passing of time."[29]

After Salpointe's unsuccessful attempts to transform and dissolve the Penitente Brotherhood into the Third Order of St. Francis, the policies of his successors in the last part of the nineteenth century and early years of the twentieth century could be described as noninterfering. Although some additional rules were supposedly issued, the archbishops of New Mexico during this period continued to denounce public acts of penance and to threaten offenders with denial of the sacraments and the impossibility of becoming godparents. Enforcement of these policies, however, was left to the parish priests.

These same years, 1894–1947, for the Brotherhood in New Mexico were also characterized by an increase in attention from Presbyterian, Methodist, Congregationalist, and Baptist ministers and their communities who were moving into the new U.S. Territory and, later, the new State of New Mexico (1912). Perhaps the most well known among them was Rev. Alex M. Darley, who titled himself the "apostle of the Colorado Mexicans" on the title page of his book, *The Passionists of the Southwest, or the Holy Brotherhood: A Revelation of the 'Penitentes.'*[30] Darley found the practices of the Penitente Brotherhood as the perfect platform from which he could articulate his critiques against the Roman Catholic Church. In his book, Darley blames the Roman

---

of their link to the Third Order of St. Francis, see Michael P. Carroll, *The Penitente Brotherhood: Patriarchy and Hispano-Catholicism in New Mexico* (Baltimore, MD: Johns Hopkins Press, 2002), 27–35.

[28] For more details of the ongoing struggles between the Hermandad and Salpointe over approving rules for the Brotherhood, see Weigle, *Brothers of Light,* 57–63.

[29] Ibid., 63.

[30] Darley, *The Passionists of the Southwest.*

Church of misleading its membership through the propagation of penitential practices:

> These serious seekers, by a false road, for salvation, have not been forgotten of God, ever on the watch for the sincere, even though ignorant and, therefore, false seeker for light. . . . The author desires to say, in spite of false Jesuit denunciation of them, that the members represent the sincerest followers of "Her—drunk with the blood of the saints." Papacy and Penance are a loyally married pair, and salvation sought by the latter's hard road has been, we believe, the aim of the majority of the old-time members. God's answer in the conversion of so many of them seems to prove it. Sad it is, that they knew not the "free salvation" route sooner, and sadder it is that so few care whether they are saved or not. May that only true Penitente,—Jesus Christ—reveal Himself soon, as the last to suffer for sin unto salvation.[31]

Darley did convince some Penitentes to disassociate with the Brotherhood. How many he converted is not known. From those he did convert, however, Darley was able to obtain copies of the Penitente rules and specific details concerning their penitential practices. Darley published his discoveries with the hope that more members of the Hermandad would be inspired to abandon both the Roman Church and the Penitente Brotherhood.

Thanks both to the ongoing pressure by the archbishops of Santa Fe to keep Penitente activities private and secret and to the increased negative publicity of Protestant commentators such as Darley, the Penitente Brotherhood increased the level of secrecy surrounding its membership and its activities. Consequently, determining an accurate estimate of Penitente membership has been impossible. Even after extensive research into population studies and archival materials, Weigle states, "While the Brotherhood was by no means extinct then [two to three thousand in 1960], it had clearly declined dramatically from the nineteenth-century estimates of 85–95 percent of the entire Hispanic male populace."[32]

In addition, the increased secrecy served to strengthen suspicions and accusations that some of the Moradas were seeking to exert

---

[31] Ibid., 58.
[32] Weigle, *Brothers of Light*, 98.

political influence over government officials and judicial proceedings.[33] The negative, public image of the Brotherhood that these charges created, regardless of their veracity, inhibited developing more open dialogue between the Brothers and church leaders during the first half of the twentieth century. Nonetheless, as Weigle notes, the Roman Church did not accuse the Brotherhood of becoming a secret society in the same way it branded the Masons.

At the same time, within the Brotherhood there was a growing number of members, led by Don Miguel Archibeque, interested in organizing the Moradas in New Mexico and southern Colorado into one association and affecting a "reconciliation" with the Catholic Church.[34] This process began during the time when Rudolph Aloysius Gerken was the archbishop of the Archdiocese of Santa Fe (1933–1943), but didn't come to fruition until the time that Edwin Vincent Byrne was leading the archdiocese (1943–1963). In 1943, Archibeque approached the new archbishop about reconciling the Hermandad with the church. Amenable to Archibeque's invitation, Archbishop Byrne, in 1946, approved a new set of rules for the Hermandad with the stipulation that they be accepted unanimously by all of the Moradas. Although Archibeque was not able to obtain unanimous approval, Byrne issued a statement in early 1947 announcing the creation of the Archbishop's Supreme Council, with Archibeque named as the first Hermano Supremo Arzobispal.

The archbishop's statement of 1947 included a declaration with four parts. The first sought to clarify the official status of the Brotherhood, saying, "That the Association of Hermanos de Nuestro Señor Jesús Nazareno is not a fanatical sect apart from the church, as some seem to think, but an association of Catholic men united together in love for the passion and death of our Blessed Lord and Saviour."[35] Second, he defended the Brothers' practice of "corporal and spiritual penance," maintaining that it was mandated by Jesus himself as a "necessity" for salvation and that the Hermandad "descended from those Tertiaries founded here by the Franciscans in centuries gone by."[36]

---

[33] For an exploration of Penitente political involvement in New Mexico, see Weigle, "Secular Aspects of the Territorial Period," in *Brothers of Light*.

[34] "Reconciliation" is the word that Weigle uses to describe what the Brothers sought with the Catholic Church. See Weigle, *Brothers of Light*, 106.

[35] Ibid., 227.

[36] Ibid.

In the third part of his declaration, Byrne defined the nature of the Hermanos' penitential activities as being rid of excesses, and as being neither sadistic nor masochistic. Nonetheless, the archbishop affirmed the position of previous archbishops that their penitential practices must be done in moderation and in private, so as to avoid scandal and pride. He added, though, that outsiders must respect the privacy of the Hermanos and should not intrude on their activities.

In the fourth and last part of his 1947 statement and declaration, Byrne reminded the Penitentes, "That we have the authority and power to suppress this association, just as we can and must suppress any other pious association in the church which goes counter to, or exceeds, the laws of God and His church, or the dictates of reason. But if the Brethren proceed with moderation and privately and under our supervision, meanwhile giving a good example to all as Catholics and citizens, they have our blessing and protection."[37]

Archbishop Byrne's official recognition and approval of the Penitente Brotherhood in 1947 changed the relationship between the Hermanos and church officials. Since 1833, when Padre Martínez of Taos and Bishop Zubiría of Durango voiced their disapproval of the public penitential practices of the Hermandad, the activities of the Brothers had been under close scrutiny. When Roman Catholic officials couldn't disband the Brotherhood or reshape it into the Third Order of St. Francis, they sought vigorously to remove the penitential activities from the public eye. The secretiveness that the Roman officials prescribed made the Brotherhood even more enticing and mysterious to Protestant missionaries, investigative reporters, and curious tourists.[38] After surviving 114 years of dissension between the Hermandad and church officials, the Brothers not only achieved official church approbation but also initiated and successfully established a council through

---

[37] Ibid., 208. Originally in *Santa Fe New Mexican,* January 29, 1947.

[38] In 1936 Carl N. Taylor, a journalist for *Today Magazine,* was murdered in New Mexico. Taylor was doing research on the Penitentes and had reportedly taken pictures of the Brothers while they were flagellating themselves. Although the case was never solved, the Penitentes became associated with the murder. In 1937 Roland Price directed a movie called *The Lash of the Penitentes,* in which he claims to tell the story of Taylor's murder by the Penitentes in documentary style. For more details, see Pulido, *The Sacred World,* 51–53; and Weigle, *Brothers of Light,* 105–10.

which the Hermanos and the archdiocesan administrators would have regular contact.

CONCLUDING REMARKS

The history of the Penitentes of northern New Mexico and southern Colorado is a complicated one—one that surely cannot be completely captured in a few pages. Furthermore, it continues into the present day. As the story of the copper medallion indicates, the Penitentes themselves are struggling to renarrate a past that authorizes their evolving present. Numerous scholars have sought to establish the origins of the Penitente Brotherhood, only to admit in the end that we do not know—and are not likely to ever know the precise origins of the Hermandad. In chapter 4 we return to this question about the origins of the Brotherhood, but by examining the way in which Larry constructs their story and why that's important to them.

My intention here is not to take one more look at all the evidence available and to draw new conclusions about how and why the European settlers in New Mexico began performing penitential practices. I will leave those questions for historians to pursue. Should we ever discover more precise details about the origin and development of these penitential practices in New Mexico, our questions about the effects of these practices on the participants would remain. What we do know and what we have presented in this chapter is that the Hermandad in this area has survived for nearly two hundred years, despite the criticisms of religious leaders, both Roman Catholic and Protestant. Even papal orders have not succeeded in disbanding the Hermandad.

Two observations are worth noting here. The first relates to the noticeable increase of secrecy that has come to surround Penitente practices. That secrecy has developed for several reasons. The primary reason is that the bishops and archbishops of the area have mandated the Brothers keep their practices secret. As we saw in this chapter, making the practices private was not sufficient. Beginning with Lamy and continuing to the present day, one of the responsibilities of the Hermandad is to "observe secrecy on activities concerning Hermano matters."[39] Equally significant, the Penitentes and their activities have received substantial and widespread attention over the past decades by church leaders, historians, sociologists, artists, religion scholars,

---

[39] Taken directly from "Responsibilities of the Hermandad," distributed by the archbishop for Lent 2001.

and investigative reporters. A considerable amount of that attention has been negative and has resulted in the Brothers wanting to keep certain aspects of their spiritual practices secret, or at least private. While understandable, this veil of secrecy has also made access to the Brotherhood nearly impossible for those sympathetic to their way of life. We should also note that it's ironic that the Roman Catholic bishops were prescribing secrecy at the same time they were concerned with secret societies.

The second thing we should highlight here is Archbishop Lamy's 1856 directive to screen candidates for membership in the Brotherhood. Lamy decreed that anyone who was a recent criminal or who was guilty of "vices" was prohibited from membership. If the intention of the Hermandad is to do penance for personal sins and the sins of others, this decree appears out of place. Unless, of course, there are differences in the way their practices are viewed within the context of the spiritual life. We return to this topic in the last chapter of this work.

As noted in this chapter, we have some sense of the historical events that have shaped the Penitentes and their practices over the years. This book explores how the practices of the Penitentes have shaped them. While issues of access continue to exist, the Penitentes promise to be powerful conversation partners for theologians wishing to explore how spiritual practices shape their practitioners and their communities.

The Morada in Arroyo Seco is presently one of the most active within the Brotherhood and one of the least written about in Penitente scholarly literature. In this chapter I sought to introduce the reader not only to the Hermandad and its history, but also to the Penitentes of Seco. My intention is to document the activities of the Brotherhood in Seco. Another is to hear some of the people who participate in the penitential rituals and to understand more fully their experiences. In the following chapters, we will pursue our goal of documentation, adding to the amount of primary materials available for future research, and we will enter into conversation with some of the participants. In chapter 2 we'll take a closer look at the variety of practices that the Penitentes perform during Holy Week.

Holy Week in Arroyo Seco

INTRODUCTORY REMARKS

Doing This for God

As the Auxiliadoras (women's auxiliary) were in the kitchen of the Morada preparing and rewarming their Good Friday meal of creamed spinach, salmon patties, and pinto beans, and as I was thinking about what I would say in the dinner blessing, a pregnant woman in her midtwenties started talking to me. She told me that she was very tired, but also very happy that she was able to attend the Penitente Encuentro and Lenten meal at the Morada. For many years she had been participating in these events, she explained. This year, however, in order to attend the events of the day, she had to rearrange her work schedule at the bakery and take the night shift on Thursday. The bakery was extremely warm that night and she decided to keep the door open. She told me that she had started to become afraid with the door open, but then thought that because she was doing this for God, he would keep her safe.

In this chapter we will outline the activities of the Penitentes during Holy Week and take a closer look at the particular event mentioned by the young woman, El Encuentro, which means "encounter" or "the encounter" in Spanish. In this context it refers specifically to the encounter between Jesus and his mother, Mary, as Jesus carries his cross. As we'll see, there are many different ways in which people participate in these events. Some play particular roles in the dramas. Others prepare and serve the meals that are provided between the services. Others are responsible for logistical concerns. Among the participants there are men and women, children and adults, parishioners and visitors, laypeople and clergy. My assumption is that there is no single way in which all of these participants experience these activities. In fact, I am assuming that each of the participants, as they continue their engagement with the Penitente activities, will construct and reconstruct the ways in which they interpret the significance of these events for their lives.

While the greater part of this chapter is devoted to the structure of Holy Week events, I do not want the people who are participating in these events to disappear. This is the reason we begin and conclude this chapter with comments from two women who participate in the Good Friday events in Seco, and who do so in very different ways. Their stories are also very different. We open the chapter with the story about a pregnant woman who has been participating in the Encuentro and the Lenten meal for many years. This particular year she had to rearrange her work schedule in order to participate. This young woman sees her participation in the Good Friday Penitente events as "something she does for God." God does something for her too; God provides protection for her and the child she is carrying. Participation in these particular Good Friday events is part of her relationship with God. Of all the events that take place that day within the parish community, these two are the ones she identifies as part of her relationship with God. At the end of this chapter we'll hear from another woman, who is not a member of the parish. Neither does she call herself Christian, but she too has a significant connection with the Penitente Encuentro.

The Participants

Even after gaining the official approval in 1947 by the Roman Catholic Church in New Mexico, the Hermandad has continued to decline in membership. Many Penitente Moradas have closed over the years, after serving for decades as spiritual focal points for both the Hermanos and the surrounding villages. Most of the surviving Moradas of New Mexico have accepted the rules established by the archdiocese and have become members of the Archbishop's Supreme Council, better known presently as the Mesa Directiva. There continue to be variations from Morada to Morada in the ways in which the Hermanos perform their spiritual practices, but the possibility of seeing public Holy Week processions of men in their underwear (en paños menores), wearing black hoods (vendas) over their heads, dragging heavy wooden crosses (maderos), or flagellating themselves with whips (disciplinas) made of yucca strips or sisal fibers no longer exists. Whatever penitential practices the Penitentes continue to perform, they performed them either inside the meeting room of the Morada or in a secluded area outside their Morada—late at night or before sunrise.

What remained public of the Penitente Holy Week activities was a variety of events that commemorated and ritually reenacted particular moments from the final days of the life of Jesus. These events, which formed part of a larger, yearly calendar of rituals and events, took the form of processions, folk dramas, and prayer services that were performed on Wednesday, Thursday, and Friday of Holy Week.[1] Since each Morada has its own repertoire, depending on the traditions of that particular community, there is not a uniform schedule of services. Even after several Holy Week visits I have not experienced all of the services performed in Seco because there are so many. Some of the events overlap.

Among the participants there were the Penitentes, the Auxiliadoras, the Verónicas, other members of the parish, the pastor, and guests from the local community and the surrounding areas. The Penitentes, with the exception of one, were all men. The male Penitentes participated in a variety of ways. Some led prayers and had speaking parts during the Holy Week dramas. Others carried and changed the clothing of the statue of Jesus. Others portrayed particular people in the dramas. Some played the Roman guards, who watched as Jesus hung on the cross. Another played the blind man, chosen by a Roman guard to pierce the side of Jesus. Another played Joseph of Arimathea, who took the body of Jesus and put it in a tomb. Other Brothers were responsible for guiding the movement or procession of the Brothers among the various sites of the dramas: from the Morada to the church plaza; from the church to the plaza; and from the plaza back to the Morada. Processing to and from the Morada entailed crossing the road that leads to the Taos Ski Valley and required two brothers to stop traffic in both directions.

The Madre Cuidadora helped carry the statue of Mary during El Encuentro and assisted the Verónicas in performing their responsibilities. She is one of two women in New Mexico who are Penitentas. Some years ago she was given membership in honor of her long-term leadership as Madre Cuidadora[2] of the Verónicas. The Verónicas, named after the legendary woman one of them portrayed, were teenage girls, thirteen years of age or older, who helped carry the statue of Mary during El Encuentro and performed other parts in the drama

---

[1] Marta Weigle refers to the folk dramas as "dramatic tableaux." William Wroth describes them as processions, into which the medieval tradition of passion plays has been incorporated. In Arroyo Seco, Larry Torres refers to them as "sacred dramas" and "folk dramas."

[2] The mother nanny.

throughout Good Friday. One portrayed Veronica, which means "true icon" in Greek, who was the woman who wiped the face of Jesus with a cloth while he carried the cross. She then showed all those gathered the image of Jesus' face that was retained by the cloth. Another played Mary, the mother of Jesus, as she received the crown of thorns and the nails after Jesus' body was removed from the cross.

The pastor was also among the participants. In the events that the Penitentes led, the priest did not have a leadership role. He participated as a member of the wider parish community. Like them, the priest didn't attend all of the Penitente services and all of the official parish services. Throughout Holy Week, members of the parish community came and went. A small number of the parishioners attended all or most of the services during the week. The majority of people selected from among the Penitente and official parish services.

The visitors composed the last group of participants. In Arroyo Seco, this group was often rather large because Larry invited adult students from the University of New Mexico in Albuquerque to attend the Good Friday Penitente services. A few chose to attend the official Good Friday service in the church that afternoon, but most of them walked around the village at that time. These visitors arrived by bus on Friday morning, just before the Encuentro began. They stayed until after El Sermón del Descendimiento (the sermon on Jesus' body being removed from the cross). After the Encuentro, Larry offered them a lecture on the village of Arroyo Seco and the Penitente practices. Following the lecture and before the events of the afternoon, Larry's mother and sisters provided lunch for the invited guests.

OVERVIEW OF THE HOLY WEEK SCHEDULE

Below is the Holy Week schedule in Arroyo Seco, based on the Passion Sunday bulletin of Holy Trinity Parish in 1999, and my own notes. I have included all the events of which I am aware. I have given a brief description of the event and the location where the service took place. As the opening story suggests, El Encuentro, which takes place on Good Friday morning, is one of the central rituals of the week. For that ritual I have chosen to provide a more detailed description.

Wednesday

Most of the active Penitentes in Seco took off from work for the end of Holy Week, arrived at the Morada on Wednesday afternoon, and remained there through all the events of Friday. They returned to their homes on Saturday, around 2:00 or 3:00 a.m. There were no beds in the Morada; the members either slept on the bancos (ledges made of mud built into the mud walls of the Morada) or on the dirt floor. The bancos lined the walls of the large, private meeting room of the Morada.

5:00 p.m. The Hermanos, along with their wives, girlfriends, and guests, began the three days of events with the celebration of the Mass and a common dinner in the Morada. The women told me that they cook the food in their homes and then reheat the meal on the gas stove in the Morada. The Brothers didn't install electricity in the Morada until 2003. After the common meal was over, the women and children returned to their homes. Most of the Brothers remained there for the night.

Evening. The Hermanos met in the evening. Two members described these to me as "business meetings." These meetings included the approval of new members and auxiliary members, the initiation of new members, and the election of new officers. The minimum age for membership was raised during the years of my research. Formerly, Roman Catholic males, fifteen years of age or older, were eligible for membership. Presently, the age is set at twenty-one. Auxiliary membership is also possible. On one visit I met a twelve-year-old boy who was an auxiliary member.

Holy Thursday
During the day the Hermanos remained at the Morada and continued with their meetings and processes of initiation.

7:00 p.m. Mass of the Lord's Supper (Holy Trinity Church). The Hermanos, their families, and the Verónicas processed from the Morada, down the street, and into the "new" parish church for the celebration of the Mass. Led by a kerosene lantern, the Hermanos walked in pairs and sang alabados as they processed. The alabados are songs of praise sung in a seventeenth-century dialect of Spanish that have been handed down from one generation of Hermanos to the next. The two men in front led the singing from a cuaderna (book) in which the words were handwritten. They sang the stanzas, to which the other members responded with the antiphon. Four Hermanos carried a small wooden platform on which a wooden statue of Jesus (about forty inches tall) was secured. On this night Jesus was dressed in a purple cloak with a white tunic underneath. Behind Jesus the Verónicas carried another platform with the statue of Our Lady of Sorrows (Mary, the mother of Jesus) clothed in a blue dress. The Verónicas accompanied the statue of Mary throughout the various celebrations. They wore black dresses, stockings, and veils. Each of the three years I attended there were four Verónicas. The Auxiliadoras followed the Verónicas and the statue of Mary in the procession. The Brothers placed the statues of Mary and Jesus in the church sanctuary where all could see them.

This celebration of the Mass on Holy Thursday (approximately two hours) commemorates the Last Supper of Jesus with his disciples. Customarily, the celebration is a Mass with several additions. After the homily, there is the washing of feet, commemorating Jesus' washing of his disciples' feet. After Communion there is a procession of the Eucharist to a place of repose and eucharistic adoration for several hours, commemorating Jesus' going with his disciples to the Mount of Olives to pray on the night before he died.

In Arroyo Seco the Hermanos led the community in singing alabados during the Mass where there is customarily a hymn from their hymnbook. On some occasions, an Hermano used the overhead projector to flash the antiphons from the alabado on the church wall. The Hermanos sang the stanzas and the congregation responded with the antiphon. Apart from the alabados and parts of the eucharistic prayer, the Mass was in English. For the washing of the feet the pastor chose twelve people to have their feet washed by him. The three times that I have attended this service in Arroyo Seco the pastor chose twelve Hermanos. After Communion, the priest carried the Eucharist and led a procession across the church plaza and into the old church. The statues of Jesus and Mary were also taken to the old church. The Eucharist was placed on the altar in the center of the church, and the statues were taken up into the old sanctuary.

After the Eucharist was incensed and there was a brief moment of adoration, the priest and other vested ministers left the church. Members of the community remained in prayer before the Eucharist, while some of the Hermanos joined the Verónicas and processed the statue of Mary back to the Morada.

10:00 p.m. El Prendimiento de Nuestro Padre Jesús Nazareno (the Apprehension of Our Father Jesus of Nazareth), which was performed in La Santísima Trinidad Church, is "an ancient drama re-enacting the hours of agony that our Lord spent in the Garden of Gethsemani until his betrayal by Judas Iscariot and arrest by Roman authorities."[3] The Hermanos assembled again in the church for the final event of the evening. Some of the members of the community had remained in the church since the beginning of adoration. Others left and returned in time for this reenactment. The priest returned and took a seat with the other members of the community. The Hermano Mayor led those present in a series of Our Fathers and Hail Marys in Spanish. Following the prayers, two Hermanos took off Jesus' purple garment. They also blindfolded him and bound his hands to the cross that rested upon his shoulders. After singing an alabado about Jesus in the garden, the Hermanos processed back to the Morada, singing. One Hermano told me that they left the statue of Jesus there in the church alone overnight just as Jesus was abandoned by his disciples after his arrest in the Mount of Olives.

Good Friday

Early a.m. The Brothers processed to their Calvario (Calvary) and performed acts of penance, particularly flagellation. Each year, the Brothers establish a secluded place nearby the Morada that will become their Calvario during Holy Week. This is one of those details that they keep private. One Brother said that they borrow a nearby cow pasture for their Calvario. Another said it is on the Morada grounds, near their outdoor altar.

7:00 a.m. Parishioners of Holy Trinity Parish gathered at the village churches of Arroyo Hondo, San Cristóbal, Las Colonias, and Valdez to begin their pilgrimages to the Seco plaza. Holding a crucifix, one of them led the pilgrimage by foot to the Seco Plaza. In some cases, one of them carried the banner of that community. The pilgrims planned to arrive in the plaza in time for El Encuentro.

10:00 a.m. El Sermón del Encuentro (the Sermon of the Encounter) was performed. Penitentes and other parishioners referred to it as "El Encuentro." This sacred drama depicted Padre Jesús Nazareno and Nuestra Señora de los Dolores encountering one another as Jesus carried his cross. The drama began in La Santísima Trinidad Church and

---

[3] "La Semana Santa, 1998: Parroquia de la Santísima Trinidad." Parish Bulletin. Arroyo Seco, NM.

continued in the church plaza. El Sermón de Dos y Tres Caídas (the Sermon of the Two and Three Falls) was performed concurrently with El Encuentro. This sacred drama depicted the three falls of Padre Jesús as he carried his cross and included the story of Veronica wiping his face. A more detailed description of these two dramas is given in the next section of this chapter.

11:30 a.m. Larry Torres gave a lecture on the Penitentes in La Santísima Trinidad Church for the adult students visiting from the University of New Mexico, Albuquerque. All the other participants were invited to the Morada for a Lenten meal.

12:15 p.m. In the parish hall, Larry's mother and sisters provided a Lenten meal to the adult students from Albuquerque. In the dining room of the Morada, the Auxiliadoras served a Lenten meal to the Brothers, family members, and all guests. While the meal was open to the public, most of the people present were members of the parish or had some familial connection to the Brotherhood.

1:15 p.m. The Stations of the Cross were performed on the grounds of the Morada. The Penitentes, Auxiliadoras, and guests prayed the Stations of the Cross, using the life-size statues that the Brothers built and secured permanently along the perimeter of the Morada property.

2:00 p.m. The official Good Friday service of the Roman Catholic Church, the Celebration of the Lord's Passion, was celebrated according to the rites with little elaboration. The service included prostrations, the reading of the Passion, the veneration of the cross, the prayers for the world, and the distribution of Communion. The Penitentes and their families attended, along with the other members of the parish.

3:00 p.m. The pastor practiced the Divine Mercy Devotion, which honors the mercy of God and encourages followers also to be merciful. Good Friday is the first day of nine days of prayer (novena) directed for mercy. The pastor decided to add this devotion to the Good Friday schedule.

4:00 p.m. El Sermón del Descendimiento (the Sermon on the Descent), took place at the stone altar behind the Morada. In the event of snow or rain, the Brothers have performed this drama inside the old parish church. This drama is a reenactment of how Joseph of Arimathea and Nicodemus removed the body of Jesus from the cross and laid him in the sepulcher. According to Larry Torres, this drama had not been performed for over a century. The performance was revived in 1997, when a cuaderna, with the script of the drama, was found among the personal items of a deceased Hermano.

In this drama, the body of Jesus then became the Santo Entierro (the Holy Burial) that is venerated on Good Friday evening with recitation of the rosary.[4] The drama depicted Jesus being lanced in the side, his body being taken from the cross, and the burial of his body. For this event, the Penitentes used the nearly life-size crucifix above the stone altar behind the Morada. Part of the story included the Roman guards choosing a blind man to lance the side of Jesus. Upon piercing the side of Jesus, the narration said that blood and water flowed from the side of Jesus, sprayed upon the blind man, and restored his sight. The role of the blind man was played by a Penitente who was blindfolded. As they described the taking of Jesus body from the cross, one of the Penitentes removed the crown of thorns from the head of the statue and red ribbons from his hands and feet—representing the nails used to hold Jesus to the cross. The crown and ribbons were given to one of the Verónicas, who played the part of Jesus' mother, Mary.

7:00 p.m. The Penitentes led those gathered in the recitation of the Sorrowful Mysteries of the rosary inside La Santísima Trinidad Church. Those in attendance included the Penitentes, the Auxiliadoras, the Verónicas, and a few parishioners. Sometimes the pastor attends this service. The event served as the public completion of both the Good Friday events and the public portion of the Penitente activities. Following the recitation of the rosary, the Brothers presented certificates of appreciation to the Verónicas and the person in charge of their training.

11:30 p.m. The Penitentes and their invited guests perform Las Tinieblas (Tenebrae) in the Morada chapel. The service consisted of offering prayers while remembering Jesus' time among the dead, while members of the Brotherhood performed acts of penance. Those who gathered recited the Our Father, the Hail Mary, and the Apostles' Creed

---

[4] Ibid.

for the various intentions that had been submitted to the Brotherhood. The leader announced each particular intention and then led a short litany of prayers for that intention. There were seventeen sets of prayers. Within each set of prayers, several petitions were offered. As each set of intentions was completed, one of the seventeen candles from the candelabrum was extinguished and one stanza of an alabado was sung. During this service, the invited guests were seated inside the Morada chapel. The candelabrum, with the seventeen candles, was located just inside the doorway. The doors to the chapel were closed before the service. Several Hermanos, who remained inside the chapel, recited the intentions and led the recitation of the prayers. These brothers were also responsible for extinguishing the candles, which they did with their fingers. On the other side of the closed door, the other Hermanos joined in the prayers and reportedly performed acts of penance. In chapter 3 we turn to Larry's reflections on his experience of this service.

1:30 a.m. The Brothers elected new officers and completed their business meeting. After cleaning up the Morada, they returned to their homes.

EL ENCUENTRO

There can be as many as seven different services that take place on Good Friday in Seco. Among the many services that the Penitentes conduct during Holy Week, El Encuentro is probably the most widely performed ritual among all of the Moradas of the Hermandad. In Seco, it attracts the largest crowd of local parishioners and visitors. In the years I have participated in Holy Week services in Seco (1995, 1999, 2001, and 2002), approximately 125 to 150 people were present for El Encuentro. Because of its popularity among the local parishioners, they often invite friends, family members, and guests to join them at El Encuentro. Some visitors, like the adult students from the University of New Mexico, come to experience firsthand the Penitente rituals and to learn more about New Mexican culture. Others come in search of healing for themselves or for a loved one. Because of the significant attention that El Encuentro receives, I think a more thorough description of it is necessary.

By about 9:00 Good Friday morning, parishioners arrived at the church hall to begin preparing the Lenten meal of spinach, salmon loaf, pinto beans, and fruit pie that they were planning to serve to the two busloads of senior students from the University of New Mexico, Albuquerque. Shortly before 10:00 a.m. villagers began to arrive on foot at the church plaza, around which La Santísima Trinidad Church, the new Holy Trinity Church, the parish hall, and the parish rectory are situated. These villagers made pilgrimages from four of the villages surrounding Arroyo Seco. Each of these groups, which were led by one person carrying a crucifix, walked for as much as three hours in pilgrimage to the church plaza in Arroyo Seco.

Shortly after 10:00 a.m. pilgrims, Penitentes, other parishioners, the adult students, and other guests began to converge on the plaza. As the dry, cold wind swept across the unpaved plaza, dust whirled in the air. Each of the pilgrimage groups entered via a road or small path between the surrounding buildings. Some people drove to the plaza and stood along the edge of it or inside the old church waiting for everyone to arrive. I joined the pastor who waited in the plaza with the parishioners. Hermano Larry Torres invited the two busloads of adult students from Albuquerque to wait in the old church.

The last to arrive on the plaza was the Penitente procession coming from the Morada. Stopping local traffic for a few minutes, the Penitentes and the Auxiliadoras processed down the road from the Morada to the church. Led by two Penitente rezadores (reciters of the rosary) they walked two by two into the plaza as they sang a Penitente alabado. Following the Penitentes were six young girls—called Verónicas—and their Madre Cuidadora, the single female Penitenta in Seco, all wearing black dresses, shoes, and veils. Together they carried a statue of Nuestra Señora de los Dolores, who was also clad in a similar black ensemble.

As the Penitente procession reached the plaza it split in two. Most of the Hermanos, followed by a number of Auxiliadoras, one Veronica, and a few children and friends processed into the old Holy Trinity church to collect the statue of Padre Jesús Nazareno. The night before, the Penitentes had blindfolded the statue of Jesus, crowned him with a wreath of thorns, tied his arms and hands with a rope, secured a cross along his shoulders, and left him alone. Some of the villagers and Hermanos remained outside with the other Verónicas, their Madre Cuidadora, and the statue of Mary, but the pastor and I entered the church. Once the Penitentes arrived in the old church and all the pilgrims had arrived in the plaza, the Hermanos stopped singing.

But before they proceeded with the Sermón De Dos y Tres Caídas and the Sermón del Encuentro de María Santísima con Su Amado

Hijo,[5] Hermano Torres came forward and addressed those gathered inside the old church. He welcomed all of the guests and explained that what was about to happen was sacred drama and that under no circumstances were people permitted to photograph or record the performance. Should anyone attempt to do so, he added, the performance would be stopped until the situation was resolved. In addition, he summarized the storyline of the performance because he suspected that many of them (including many of the local villagers), would not understand the Spanish dialect used in the service.[6]

Then the Hermanos lined up two by two in the center of the church. Four brothers lifted the bier on which the statue of Padre Jesús Nazareno stood and entered the line near the front. Two other Hermanos grabbed the long ends of a rope that were binding Jesus' arms and hands. Hermano Torres and another Hermano stood at the lead. "¿Quis ex vobis arguet me de peccato? [San Juan 8:46],"[7] Hermano Torres began. "¿Quién de vosotros me condenar del pecado?" he repeated in Spanish. He continued,

> You have already seen and attended to that which has been practiced up until now during these passion days, how, in order to bring about, execute, and consummate the work of redemption, Jesus Christ, Our Lord, in all truth both God and Man, gave himself over to the torment, the mocking, and the slander of evil-doers. This commemorative representation has begun so that we can contemplate what He suffered on our behalf.[8]

[5] The Sermon of the Second and Third Falls and The Sermon of the Encounter of Most Holy Mary with Her Beloved Son. An exact translation of the first sermon title would be "The Sermon of Two and Three Falls." This is the way the sermon was titled in the original handwritten text.

[6] Portions of the text used in this service are provided here in English within the body of the book. The Spanish text, which is taken directly from the scripts used during the service, can be found in the footnotes. The translation is a result of the collaborative efforts of the author, Jeremy Paden, and Nasario García.

[7] Who among you will convict me of sin? (John 8:46).

[8] English translation based on the following: "Ya habéis visto y habéis atendido en lo practicado hasta aquí en estos días de pasión como por causar y ejecutar y consumir la obra de la redención, se entregó a los tormentos y a las burlas y aprobios de los malhechores, Jesucristo, nuestro Señor, Dios y Hombre verdadero. Se ha comenzado ya esta conmemorativa representación que se hace con el objeto de contemplar lo que padeció por nuestra salud espiritual."

With a loud voice Hermano Torres continued to read the Sermón De Dos y Tres Caídas, which was photocopied on red and deep purple paper. Slowly the Hermanos processed out of the church, carrying the bound and tethered Jesus. The Auxiliadoras, parishioners, and visitors joined the end of the procession. Passing through the large wooden doors and through the cemetery that surrounded the church, the procession made its way onto the dirt road that led into the church plaza. At this point Hermano Torres read,

> The one we have before our eyes, made man of Israel, the God of our forefathers or isn't this the Lord who created and put into existence the universe with all its inhabitants or is this not the Lord who carried out wickedness over the earth unleashing the waterfall floodgates of the foul abyss saving only his servant Noah with his family? Or isn't this the Lord that buried Pharaoh's army? . . . Or isn't this the Lord who through the mouth of Elijah wrapped with heavenly fire the soldiers of the king? . . . Or, last of all, isn't this the Lord the artifice of all marvels, he who at the end of the world will come in glory and majesty to judge the living and the dead because he now, at the moment, is not using his power and because he allows himself to be taken prisoner and to be led in infamy among fascinerosos [hypocritical, two-faced][9] thieves. Yes, gentlemen, thus it is the self-same God whom we have before our sight, because God became man.[10]

Just before they entered the plaza, the two men holding the front of the bier knelt to the ground, making the statue tilt dramatically forward. This was Jesus' first of three falls. Hermano Torres read,

---

[9] "Los fascinerosos" is an archaic term that is not easily translated.

[10] "El que tenemos a vista, hecho hombre de Israel el Dios de nuestros padres o no es este Señor el que creó y puso en existencia al universo con todos sus habitantes o no es este Señor el que consumada la malicia sobre la tierra, que soltó las cataratas a las compuertas del abismo inmundo, salvando únicamente a su siervo Noé con su familia? ¿O no es este Señor el que sepultó al ejército del Faraón? . . . ¿O no es este Señor el que por boca de Elías abrazó con fuego del cielo a los soldados del rey? . . . ¿O no es por último, este Señor el artífice de todas las maravilla, el que al fin del mundo vendrá en gloria y majestad a juzgar a vivos y a los muertos porque ahora no usa de su poder y porque se deja traer prisionero y conducido con la mayor infamia entre los fascinerosos ladrones? Sí señores, así es el mismo Dios el que tenemos a la vista, pues Dios se hizo hombre."

But instead through the force of sacrifices he tries to move the will of his Eternal Father, to mercy toward men, thus we see him burdened with opprobrium, among the multitudes as an object of compassion and gentleness to the sight of all. O divine Lord, for how long you have dwelt, because of man, for love of a few finesses? In such a manner we see him gentlemen, in such a manner we experience him, in such a manner they are, permit me, the excess of the evil of the infinite weight with which our Redeemer first falls to the ground.*** [11] [Although not explained in the text, the symbols *** are in the text and indicate the timing for the Hermanos to tilt the statue of Jesus.]

After a brief time of silence, the Hermano Mayor motioned for the Verónica to move next to the statue. Facing the crowd she raised into the air a white cloth on which three identical images of Jesus' face were imprinted. As she presented the images to the crowd, Hermano Torres read from the text about how Verónica was so moved with compassion for Jesus that she pushed her way through the crowd in order to wipe the sweat and dirt away from his face. And miraculously an image of Jesus' face was transferred to the cloth.

The procession continued into the plaza for only a few steps when the two men holding the front of the bier knelt for Jesus' second fall. Hermano Torres read,

> Who among you? And we, who are the cause that he should be in
> that state, still dare to imitate the Jews and condemn him to death and
> anointed by our works, we will not imitate Saint Peter who denied
> him, even though converted. Again he came to penitence and cried
> bitterly because of his ingratitude, but Saint Peter is not an example,
> it will not be enough to move the hearts to pain and distract the guilt,
> instead unrestrained malice needs for the evildoer this innocent Lamb
> and in such a manner that doubling up the weight and increasing the
> illusion, he falls again, a second time to earth.***[12]

[11] "Si no que a fuerzas de sacrificios trata de mover la voluntad de su Eterno Padre, a misericordia para con los hombres. Así lo vemos venir cargado de oprobios, entre la muchedumbre siendo a la vista de todos objeto de compasión y ternura. O divino Señor, ¿hasta dónde ya has habitado por amor a los hombres por amor a unas finezas? Así lo vemos señores, así lo experimentamos, así están, dejadme el exceso de la maldad que con el peso de su gravedad infinita cae por primera vez en tierra nuestro Redentor.***"

[12] "Quis ex vobis? Y nosotros que somos la causa que se vea en ese estado, nos atrevemos todavía a imitación de los Judíos a condenarlo a muerte y

The procession paused again for a moment of silence. Mingled with the sounds of the wind I could hear people crying. Hermano Torres held his head in his hand and wept.

As the procession took a few more steps, the crowd of approximately 150 pilgrims and visitors began to form a large circle around the plaza. Those in procession behind the statue of Jesus poured into the plaza and joined the circle. On the far side of the plaza another procession of Penitentes, Auxiliadoras, pilgrims, and Verónicas with their Madre Cuidadora accompanied the statue of Nuestra Señora into the center of the plaza. Just before Nuestra Señora de los Dolores and Padre Jesús Nazareno had their encounter, the two Hermanos holding the front of the bier knelt for Jesus' third fall. Hermano Torres raised his voice and, with tears streaming down his face, he read,

> They pursue him and they are not moved to compassion and gentleness, to an expression so filled with feeling, their spirits pay no heed to the other words with which they scold the Jews and that happens on behalf of the discourse. "Quis ex vobis?"

> Here the hearts still respond with their evil affections and wills saying that he is an evildoer that his deed and his words are impure and blasphemous. In this way, the sinner will continue in his vice-ridden inclinations, until he turns his evil into a vicious habit. See here tripled and multiplied the weight of the burden of your sins, thus he fell a third time *** and he would remain even more downtrodden and humbled, with even more signs of being a servant, this divine Lord.[13]

---

ungido con nuestras obras, no imitaremos a San Pedro que negó convertido. Nuevamente vino a penitencia y pasó a llorar amargamente su ingratitud pero no es ejemplo de San Pedro, no será bastante para mover los corazones a dolor y distracción de las culpas, antes de la desenfrenada malicia adquiere del malhechor este inocentísimo Cordero y de tal suerte que doblando el peso y aumentando la ilusión, vuelve a caer por segunda vez en tierra.***"

[13] "Le persiguen y no se mueven a compasión y ternura, a expresión tan llena de sentimiento, no hacen caso a impresión los ánimos a las otras palabras con que reprenden a los Judíos que pasa por apoyo del discurso. 'Quis ex vobis?'

Aquí responderán todavía los corazones con sus malos afectos y malas voluntades diciendo que es un malhechor a que sus obras y sus palabras son impatías y son blasfemias. De este modo continuará el pecador en sus viciadas inclinaciones, hasta constituir hábito vicioso en sus maldades. He aquí triplicado y multiplicado el peso de la gravedad de tus culpas que por eso cayó

Another moment of silence was observed. All I could hear was the wind blowing and people weeping. The dust swirled across the plaza as the wind lifted it from the ground. As the procession with the statue of Padre Jesús Nazareno resumed and moved toward the center of the plaza, the procession with the statue of Mary also resumed and moved toward the plaza center. At the same time, the ring of participants around the plaza also began to move to the center of the plaza. The women, who were cooking the Lenten meal, came out of the church hall and joined the gathering.

As the statues were slowly brought to face each other, the Sermón De Dos y Tres Caídas moved seamlessly into the Sermón del Encuentro de María Santísima con Su Amado Hijo. One of the other Hermanos, who was leading the Marian procession, had already begun to read from Sermón del Encuentro. Shortly after Jesus' second fall, however, Hermano Torres and the other Hermano shifted from reading at the same time to reading interchangeably. Although both texts spoke with the voice of John the Evangelist, the voice of John was more clearly articulated in the Sermón del Encuentro. In the voice of the Evangelist, the other Hermano read just after Jesus' second fall,

> And seeing such a wounded, afflicted and tortured Lord, moved by natural compassion and cruelty, she came (that is Cruelty) to where I was accompanied by a ferocious man named Fury, son of a bad woman, it is said she was very loose, and each had fire sparking out of their eyes and had a terrible countenance. They said to me in a frightening scream: What does the predator do to the one who cries here? And both lifting their hands, they wanted to hurt me, but I remained alone in bitterness, because at the same time the voices of the executioners could be heard because the Lord had fallen a second time under the weight of the cross and Cruelty and Fury went so that they could lift him up again and continue his walk and upon hearing what I said, that noble woman named Compassion came to me, with the venerable elders that accompanied her, normally called Pain and Weeping.[14]

---

por tercera vez *** y quedaría más abatido y humillado con más señales de siervo, este divino Señor."

[14] "Y viendo tan lastimado y afligido y atormentado Señor, movido de natural compasión y crueldad, vino adonde estaba yo acompañado de un hombre fiero llamado Furor, hijo de una mala mujer que se decía era desenfrenada, y el uno al otro centellando llamas por los ojos y con un aspecto terrible. Me dieron un formidable grito diciendo: '¿Qué hace aquí el rapaz de que llora?'

When the moment of the "encounter" arrived, the crowd pressed in close to the statues and their followers. Some members of the gathering knelt on the dusty pavements. Others bowed their heads. The Hermano Mayor motioned to the Madre Cuidadora, the Verónicas, and the Hermanos to bring the statues face to face. Kneeling once again, the Hermanos tilted the statue of Padre Jesús. The Verónicas also knelt and tilted the statue of Nuestro Señora de los Dolores toward the statue of Padre Jesús Nazareno so that the two statues rested against each other cheek to cheek. As the encounter occurred, Hermano Torres read, first in the voice of Jesus and then in the voice of the Evangelist,

> Come afflicted Mother, come take part in the painful afflictions of the only Son of your bowels. But wait a while, look at him for whom you sigh, look at what the ungratefulness of his people has done to him. Look at what they have made of him! . . .
>
> Look upon me merciful one and attend to me benign one, give me the light of your knowledge and concede unto me the flame of your heart and temple because I have received you through the sacrament and may I die with the help of your Mother. Give me the last breath of my life among these bitter wounds so that I may love you forever in heaven.[15]

For a brief moment, then, the encounter between Jesus and Mary was observed with silence. Some of the Hermanos and Auxiliadoras

---

Y levantando ambos las manos, quisieron herirme, pero quedé sólo en amargura, porque al mismo tiempo levantan las voces los verdugos porque cayó El Señor por segunda vez con el peso de las Cruz y acudieron La Crueldad y El Furor para que del mismo modo que antes, lo levantaran, y que prosiguiese su camino y estando oyendo lo que he dicho, se llegaron a mí, aquella noble señora llamada Compasión, con los venerables ancianos que la acompañaban, comúnmente llamados Dolor y Llanto."

[15] "Llegad, llegad madre afligidísima a tomar parte de las penosas aflicciones del Hijo único de tus entrañas. Pero detente un poco, miradlo como lo han puesto las ingratitudes de su pueblo por quien tanto suspiras. ¡Cómo lo han puesto! . . .

Miradme misericordioso y atendedme benigno, dándome la luz de vuestro conocimiento y concededme las llamas de vuestro amor y templo por recibiros sacramentado y que muera con la asistencia de vuestra madre. Dadme la última respiración de mi vida entre estas amargosas llagas para eternamente amaros en la gloria."

were crying. Others appeared somber. The Verónicas struggled to keep the statue steady while making sure that their veils didn't blow away with the wind. As I contemplated the scene I kept thinking about the family next to me who were praying for their daughter. She was in her thirties and had suffered a series of strokes. They had brought her to the Encounter in hopes of a healing.

As the Hermanos and the Verónicas slowly separated the statues and backed away from one another, Hermano Torres began to read, in the voice of Jesus and with great anguish,

> Why did you come here, my dove, my love, my mother? Your pain increases my pain, and your torments torment me. Turn around, my mother, go back to your home [posada], for the company of murderers and thieves does not belong to your virginal purity. If you want to do it, great will be the pain of both of us. I will stay, to be crucified for the world. But this duty does not pertain to you and your innocence does not deserve this torment. Turn around, my mother, go back to your home, back to the ark until the floodwaters cease falling. For here you will not find where to rest your feet. There you will descend into prayer and contemplation. Comfortable and lifted up upon yourself, and you will pass through as best you can this pain, according to the will of your heavenly Father.[16]

Bringing the Sermón del Encuentro to a close, the Hermano responded to Jesus, reading in the voice of the Virgin,

> Why do you send me from this place? You know, my Lord and my God that in your presence, everything is permitted me and that there is no place to pray except in your presence. How can I separate you without separating myself from me? God has so possessed my soul that outside of him, I can do nothing. I can go nowhere without you, and

---

[16] "¿Para qué viniste aquí, paloma mía, querida mía y madre mía? Tu dolor acrecenta mi dolor y tus tormentos me atormentan a mí. Vuélvete madre mía, vuélvete a tu posada, que no pertenece a tu pureza virginal, compañía de homicidios y ladrones. Si lo queréis hacer, grave ha de ser el dolor de ambos. Quedaré yo, para ser crucificado por el mundo. Pues a ti no te pertenece este oficio y tu inocencia no merece este tormento. Vuélvete madre mía, vuélvete a tu posada, a la arca hasta que cesen las aguas del diluvio. Pues aquí no hallarás dónde descansen tus pies. Allí bajarás a la oración y contemplación. Acostumbrada y levantada sobre ti misma, y pasarás como puedas este dolor según la voluntad de tu padre celestial."

there is absolutely no way in which I can hope or receive consolation unless I am with you? I have all of my heart and all of my habitation [morada] in you, my life depends on you, because for nine months you were in the habitation [morada] of my bowels. How can I, then, not have you? For these three days if you do not receive me inside you, I will die crucified and crucified I will be buried. I will drink the bile and vinegar, I who am daughter of Adam and along with you will I breathe my last.

Goodbye, goodbye, my Jesus, goodbye beautiful Nazarene, more pure than snow and more red than ivory. Remember me mercifully as the good thief crucified with you.[17]

Following the Encounter, the Hermano Mayor stepped forward, knelt down on the dirt pavement, and led all gathered in a series of prayers and litanies in Spanish. While some of the other Hermanos also knelt, many of them remained standing with the other participants. At the conclusion of the prayers, Hermano Torres spoke briefly of the history and significance of this rite and those that would follow in the afternoon. He reminded the crowd that these rites were "sacred drama" and that no photography of any kind was permitted.

As the invited senior students from Albuquerque returned to the old church for an hour lecture about the Penitentes by Hermano Torres, half of the Hermanos led a procession with the statue of Padre Jesús Nazareno back into the church, where they planned to resume their rituals later in the afternoon. After they positioned the statue of Jesus back in the sanctuary, they returned to the Morada. The other half of the Hermanos led a procession with the statue of Nuestra Señora de

---

[17] "¿Por qué mandas alejarme de ese lugar? Tú sabes, Señor mío y Dios mío que en tu presencia, todo me es lícito y que no hay otra oración si no donde tú estás? ¿Cómo puedo yo apartarme de ti sin apartarme de mí? De tal manera tiene Dios ocupado mi corazón que fuera de él, ninguna cosa puedo hacer a ninguna parte puedo ir sin ti, y de ningún modo puedo esperar ni puedo recibir consolación en ti? Tengo todo mi corazón y dentro del tuyo tengo hecha mi morada y mi vida toda depende de ti, pues por espacio de nueve meses tu vites en mis entrañas por morada. ¿Cómo no puedo yo tener por estos tres días si allí dentro me recibieres, moriré crucificada y crucificada, seré sepultada? Beberé de la hiel y vinagre, yo que soy hija de Adán y juntamente contigo expiraré.

"Adiós, adiós, Jesús mío, adiós Nazareno hermoso más cándido que la nieve y más rojo que el marfil. Acordaos misericordia de mí como del buen ladrón crucificado contigo."

los Dolores back to the chapel of the Morada. As each procession arrived back at the Morada they knelt in the chapel and prayed. Once concluded, they joined their guests for the Good Friday meal, which the Auxiliadoras had prepared. The Good Friday meal was open to the public and consisted of chile, salmon loaf, spinach, torta de huevos (egg dumplings in chile sauce), mashed potatoes, salad, bread, sheet cakes, and Jell-O salads.

The day was far from over. There were still five more services scheduled that Good Friday: the Stations of the Cross, the official Good Friday liturgy of the church, the Sermón del Descendimiento de Nuestro Padre Jesús, the recitation of the rosary, and Las Tinieblas. The Hermanos didn't expect to return to their homes until 3:00 a.m. Saturday.

COMMENTS ON EL ENCUENTRO

Authority and Supposed Reconciliation

The sacred dramas of the Penitentes performed in the village of Seco are not what they used to be. El Encuentro no longer includes, as it did in the first half of the twentieth century, the Penitentes putting black hoods over their heads, dressing in white undergarments, and whipping themselves until they bleed.[18] The rules of the archdiocese have been successful at making sure that any such activity is done privately. The Hermandad also doesn't tie one of its members to a cross and hang him on it until he passes out from lack of oxygen. That practice was discontinued some time in the mid-twentieth century. The performance of the sacred dramas, nonetheless, continues to have intensity about it and continues to attract the attention of parishioners and guests.

I had been an ordained Roman Catholic priest for nearly three years when I visited Arroyo Seco during Holy Week of 1995. The pastor, Father Vincent Chávez, a seminary classmate and friend, invited me to

---

[18] This is the way that Isaac L. Udell portrayed the activities of the Penitentes in the early part of the twentieth century. Udell treated the wounds that the Penitentes in Taos incurred through their flagellation and other penitential practices. Udell reportedly received the permission from the Penitentes to watch some of their activities and to do a series of paintings based on his treatment of their bodies, their personal testimonies, and his eyewitness accounts. Udell depicted thirteen scenes on canvas. The paintings are now held in a private collection. At present, they are not on public display. See the gallery at the end of this book.

go out and preach the Holy Week services for him. Equally interested in ritual things, he knew he could lure me across the country with the promise that I could experience Holy Week with the Penitentes in his parish. The statues robed in human clothes, the haunting melodies of the alabados, or thoughts about the Hermanos' secret practices of penance, including ritual cutting on their backs and flagellation weren't what lingered in my mind after my first encounter with Penitente spirituality. What compelled me to return in 1999 was the fact that these practices—which appeared to be an integral part of the life of this parish community—were performed by parishioners, without the assistance, guidance, or even permission of the pastor. I was moved that Good Friday 1995, when I saw the Hermanos, the Madre Cuidadora, and the Verónicas bring the statues of Our Lady of Sorrows and Jesus face to face in the Arroyo Seco plaza for one final embrace before Jesus was led off to his death. The gathering of over one hundred people intuitively encircled the two statues to witness this intimate moment between a mother and her son, through the gentle movement of the two statues, which brought tears to my eyes, as it did to others present. But what has kept me thinking about the Penitentes in the weeks and years since was the power that the laity manifested in this small New Mexican village, nestled between the Carson National Forest and the Taos Pueblo lands.

After El Encuentro was finished on Good Friday of 1995, as the Hermanos and the parishioners processed back down the street to the Morada with their statue of Our Lady of Sorrows, Vince and I went into the rectory. Vince took off his silver-belly Resistol cowboy hat, which he wore every day with his black Wrangler jeans, black boots, and black clerical shirt. He questioned out loud, "I wonder why they never even asked me for a blessing? I was standing there the whole time in my clerics." Although I hadn't thought of it that way, I knew what Vince meant. The Penitentes didn't need us priests to be there. It was clear to both of us that this performance would have happened whether we were there or not.

Perhaps his response was indicative of a young priest and newly installed pastor who was seeking to locate his position in this parish community. I suspect, however, he was exploring something else in his questioning. If this had been the recitation of the rosary, something that could happen on any given day in a parish community, we would have thought nothing of it. He wouldn't have considered providing any kind of ritual leadership or providing any indication of authorization. But this very public performance of scenes from the life of Jesus and Mary, which energized the parishioners of his community to rise early that morning and walk several miles in pilgrimage through the New Mexican countryside, attracted two busloads of adult students from the University of New Mexico, Albuquerque, and had been performed in the Seco church and its plaza for decades, appeared to be a powerful manifestation of the spiritual and cultural legacy of this local community. As a fellow pilgrim he was as welcome as anyone else to participate in the performances. Neither his permission nor his blessing, however, was required.

On the one hand, Vince's comments are indicative of his exploring the issues of authorization. They also go beyond those. I think, ultimately, Vince wanted to have more participation in the Penitente activities. I interpret his question as asking, "Why didn't they ask me to make a contribution to the performance?" I see his response as indicative of the larger, ongoing rupture in the relationship between the Penitentes and church leadership. There may have been "reconciliation" between the Penitentes and Archbishop Byrne in 1947, but that doesn't mean that the "deep wound" that we heard Larry describe in chapter 1 has completely healed. The supposed "reconciliation" rests on the Penitentes' conforming to the rules established by the archbishops and administered by the Mesa Directiva. The reconciliation may have been successful at finally getting the Penitentes to acknowledge the rules of the archdiocese, but it hadn't realized a deeper conversation and reflection about what the Penitentes and others experience through these practices.

Linguistic Details

Within the Hermandad there have been ongoing conversations about performing El Encuentro and the other sacred dramas of Holy Week in English, not Spanish. They are concerned about the fact that very few people are able to understand Spanish, especially the dialect that is used in northern New Mexico. Furthermore, among the men who are seeking membership in the Brotherhood, fewer and fewer are able to read and understand Spanish. Part of their novitiate now includes Spanish lessons. Many years ago Larry had already made the commitment to make his publications bilingual. For example, the booklet that he produced for Las Posadas has Spanish on one page and English on the other. In addition, the guidebook and commitment form he created for the Verónicas has the text in Spanish on the left page and English on the right. His hope is that members of the community will learn both languages. As a consequence of these linguistic shifts, Larry has also sought ways to frame and to describe for people what they will see in a performance, knowing that many won't understand the Spanish. He'll often offer more comments at the end of a performance, as noted above.[19]

One of the details in the Spanish text that I want to point out for our purposes occurs in the final scene of El Encuentro. After the statues of Jesus and Mary encounter one another, Jesus tells his Mother to leave him because seeing her suffer only increases his pain. Regardless of whether one understands the Spanish text at this point in the performance, the tone of Larry's voice in combination with the movement of the statues makes it clear. Slowly, the Verónicas and the Hermanos separate the two statues as the anguish in Larry's voice increases. The detail that could be lost for the person who cannot understand the Spanish is found in Mary's reply to Jesus' command to leave him. Mary says, "I have all of my heart and all of my habitation [morada] in you, my life depends on you, because for nine months you were in the habitation [morada] of my bowels. How can I, then, not have you? For these three days if you do not receive me inside you, I will die crucified and crucified I will be buried. I will drink the bile and vinegar, I who am daughter of Adam and along with you will I breathe my last." Mary declares to Jesus that she cannot separate herself from him. She has made a home in him because he made a home in her. And so, she will also die with him and be buried with him. As in life, they will be together in the earth. For Mary, her morada, her home, becomes a place of both life and death.

For many, if not most of the participants in the Encuentro, this particular detail passes unnoticed. In the next chapter, however, we'll see this mingling of life and death once again as Larry shares with us how he interprets Penitente spirituality at this point in his life. Like Mary, the Penitente Morada becomes his place of death and life.

Concluding Reflections

While most of those who come to El Encuentro are Roman Catholic, Christians from other denominations and people of other faith backgrounds come too. Some residents of Taos and the surrounding area

---

[19] This was also the case when I attended Las Posadas with Larry.

come because they have heard about the Penitente activities from
friends or parishioners. Others come, having heard one of Larry's
radio programs about the spirituality of the Penitentes and their activities. Mirabai Starr, a colleague of Larry's from University of New
Mexico, Taos, went to the Seco plaza on Good Friday 2003, to participate in El Encuentro. That was her second time to participate. Mirabai
and I met on Good Friday 2002, and have kept in touch regularly ever
since. Following her second Encuentro experience I asked if she would
write to me about how she experienced El Encuentro. In an e-mail, she
wrote:

> I am Jewish, by birth, and Buddhist by inclination. I am also the
> mother of a recently dead daughter and I needed to be near Mary on
> this day. I went alone to the medieval Penitente rite and stood in silence,
> wrapped close in my woolen shawl, weeping and invisible. . . . The
> elders sang and recited the ancient Spanish prayers until their aged
> voices grew hoarse. The leaders sobbed as they retraced the steps of
> Christ's passion. The prayers and songs of two groups blended in a
> dissonant beauty as they approached one another. . . . It was the en-
> counter between Mary and her son that moved me most. When at last
> the two processions connected, the effigy of Jesus was tilted toward
> the statue of His Blessed Mother in a mystical embrace and then they
> parted. You must go away from this place, Madre, the Hermanos
> chanted. You must not witness the suffering and death of your beloved
> son. And they began to move backwards then, removing Mary from
> her encounter with unspeakable loss. . . . I am not the mother of the
> Savior. I am only the mother of a fourteen year old girl named Jenny
> who died in a car accident on the Day of the Dead in 2001, just on the
> verge of her flowering into a brilliant and beautiful woman who loved
> God. I cannot bear the loss and yet I bear it. Communion with Mary
> helps. Magical Spring days in the Sangre de Cristo Mountains where
> I make a solitary pilgrimage among strangers and neighbors to witness
> the Passion of Jesus Christ and the love of His holy Mother and draw
> solace from universal and shared grief help. Mother of God, have
> mercy on me.[20]

Mirabai came to El Encuentro because she "needed to be with
Mary." Both of them have "encountered unspeakable loss." Mary
lost her son; Mirabai lost her daughter. Mirabai needs to be with her
when Mary encounters her greatest loss so that she can also draw on

[20] Mirabai Starr to author, e-mail, May 24, 2003. Used with permission.

Mary's strength. In Mary's encounter with the pending death of Jesus, Mirabai finds comfort, companionship, and strength. She sees in Mary the possibility of living, while still bearing the loss that death brings. "I cannot bear the loss, and yet I bear it," Mirabai says.

Initial plans for this research project included interviewing a sampling of the people who participate in the Holy Week services of the Penitentes. From comparing my own initial experiences with those of others, I suspected there to be a wide range of reflections. The voices of the two women we have heard in this chapter certainly indicate that. Their religious backgrounds and personal contexts are different. They do not share a similar historical connection with Penitente practices either. They are, however, both drawn to participate in El Encuentro. Their comments tell us that the experiences of the many people who participate in Penitente activities are worth further attention by theologians. In particular we may find in the specific forms of affective participation a more profound theological set of meanings and images than in official Holy Week rites or Marian devotions.

In the following chapter we'll engage another participant in a deeper, fuller way. In this chapter we encounter Larry Torres, who serves as the archivist of the Seco Morada and who has been an active member since he was nine years old. As noted above, Larry has a multilayered relationship with the Hermandad that extends beyond being an active member. Larry has published books and numerous newspaper articles about the sacred dramas and the practices performed by the Penitentes. He also speaks regularly about Penitente spirituality in his weekly radio program. In this chapter we hear how Larry presently interprets his experience of being a Penitente for more than forty years.

Chapter 3

Era y soy polvo[1]

> I remember a priest asked me once if I believed in God . . . and he was
> kind of shocked when I said I believe that there is a God . . . for those
> who need a God. Something that takes you a little while to realize . . .
> So the question is "Do you need a God?" . . . Now that is harder to
> answer than "Is there a God? Do you believe in God?"[2]

INTRODUCTION

Rev. Vincent Chávez, my seminary classmate, told me about Larry
Torres shortly after Vincent arrived in Arroyo Seco as the new pastor
of Holy Trinity Parish. He had invited me to visit Arroyo Seco during
Holy Week because he thought I would be interested in the Penitente
practices and how they were interwoven with the official rites of the
Roman Catholic Church there. During my first visit to Seco, in 1995,
Larry was in Europe, leading a group of high school students on a
tour of European cathedrals. My next visit, in 1999, Larry led another
European tour, but this time arranged his departure for the evening
of Good Friday, allowing him to be present for most of the Holy Week
events. He and his brother Patrick were video recording the activities
of the Hermandad that they performed outside and with the public. According to Larry, he had been trying for years to convince his
brother Penitentes of the importance of recording their activities for
future generations.

Vincent had explained to Larry that I was interested in researching
the practices of the Penitentes and arranged for me to interview Larry
during my Holy Week research trip. This interview on Good Friday
1999 was the beginning of my research with Larry. Over the following
six years Larry and I spent a lot of time together during my visits to
Arroyo Seco. Besides doing taped interviews and recording some of

[1] I Was and I Am Dust.

[2] Unless otherwise noted, all quotations in this chapter from Larry T. Torres,
interview by author, tape recording, Arroyo Seco, NM, December 14–16, 2002.

Larry's public speeches, I spent several days following Larry through his day. Everywhere we went in the Taos/Seco area we were approached by local people who knew Larry or who had read his most recent column or who had heard him on the radio that morning. On one occasion, while we were attending a pole climbing ritual at the Picuris Pueblo, one man came over to tell Larry about the bogey creatures that were part of his childhood. Over the summer, the radio station had been airing Larry's prerecorded segments on New Mexican culture. That particular week the topic was the bogey creatures of the Southwest, a topic that is close to Larry's heart. We discuss this later in the chapter.[3]

Out of the twenty-some active members of the Seco Morada, Larry Torres surfaced as a key informant very quickly. From the detailed account of El Encuentro in chapter 2, we can see that Larry plays a significant role in the public activities of the Penitentes in Seco. Born in 1952, Hermano Larry Torres has been a member of the Fraternidad for over forty years, which makes him one of the three most senior in membership of the Arroyo Seco Morada. Although the rules presently state that a person requesting membership in the Brotherhood must be at least twenty-one years of age, this was not always the case. Larry joined when he was nine. For the last twenty years he has been an unofficial archivist of the Seco Morada, collecting stories from the elder members of the village, researching the histories behind the Penitente activities, and making video and voice recordings whenever possible.

Besides being a longtime member of the Brotherhood in Seco, Larry is the most public member who speaks about the history and the activities of the Pentitentes in the Southwest. He has authored several books about New Mexican Hispanic culture.[4] He also has written two newspaper columns, one in Spanish, one in English, for *The Taos News*. On Wednesday mornings Larry can also be heard on the Taos solar radio station, KTAO 101.9 FM, where he discusses New Mexican culture and local events during his program: *Cafecito y Cultura*. When it

[3] For two illustrations from Larry's picture book on bogey creatures of the Southwest, see appendix 4.

[4] *Six Nuevomexicano Folk Dramas for Advent Season* (Albuquerque: University of New Mexico Press, 1999); *Los Cocos y Las Coconas: The Bogey Creatures of the Hispanic Southwest* (Arroyo Seco, NM: Larry Torres, 1995); *Los Matachines Desenmascarados: An Historical Interpretation of the Ancient Dance-drama* (Arroyo Seco, NM: Larry Torres, 1996).

became clear to me that I would focus my attention on the experiences of one Penitente, Larry became the obvious choice, but not simply because of his credentials as an Hermano or as a commentator on the life and culture of the Taos area. Indeed, his particular position as both practitioner and as cultural commentator has afforded him more practice in how to talk about secret practices publicly than other members. I chose him, however, because he chose me as a trustworthy conversation partner for reflecting on Penitente practices.

On several occasions Larry told me that other researchers from other universities had come to Seco in hopes of learning more about the Penitentes and their way of life. Rarely would he give them any information. He would invite them to participate in the public activities that they had planned, but he refused to give them any interviews or access to his archival materials. They were welcome to gather whatever information they could from the public performances, but he was not willing to provide them with any other information. On more than one occasion he commented to me that researchers from outside of the area tended to sensationalize aspects of Penitente spirituality (e.g., flagellation) because they didn't make the effort to learn the history or context of their practices. Larry was happy that I, on the other hand, was taking the initiative to understand the Penitentes in their particular historical and social contexts.

My being a Roman Catholic priest both benefited my research and posed challenges to it. Being a priest helped me to establish a connection with Larry. That connection, however, wasn't enough for him to share freely with me about what it has been like to be a Penitente. The relationship between the Penitentes and the institutional church has been difficult, if not painful at times, as we saw in chapter 1. Being a priest didn't guarantee that Larry would automatically trust me.

In discussions about prayer and issues of spirituality laypeople typically initiate the conversation with the priest. Although I was in Seco primarily as a theologian and a researcher, I was still a priest. And I was the one initiating the conversation with Larry and asking him to talk about his spiritual practices and how he experienced them. I was not only reversing the usual pattern of discussion between priest and layperson, but also asking my conversation partner to talk about a set of spiritual practices that the institutional church had condemned at one time and still treats with some level of suspicion today.

As the next section of this chapter will reveal, my being a priest influenced the project once again when I left active ministry in the middle of my research. Although the reason for my departure from Roman Catholic ministry had not been made public, it would be soon. I was, consequently, faced with the challenge of sharing my story with my key informant—a Roman Catholic layman. In the latter part of this chapter I'll address how it influenced my conversations with Larry and the overall shape of my research.

FROM TAKING NOTES TO COMPARING NOTES[5]

Over the four years that I spent doing field research in Arroyo Seco, my relationship with Larry underwent significant changes. The early stages of my fieldwork could be characterized as my seeking information about the Brotherhood, its members, and their practices. Larry was an important resource. He had both the experience and the archival material. As I noted above, a major shift occurred when I realized that ethnographic research was more than simply gathering information from a different location. I couldn't expect transparency on Larry's part if I wasn't willing to provide it myself.

I began researching the Penitentes with no experience in doing ethnographic research. I was learning how to do ethnography at the same time I was seeking to better understand the Penitentes and their practices. In the initial stages of my research I treated the field site as if it were a library. In my interviews and participant observation I went around Seco asking questions and recording ideas and comments as best I could. Every person and situation was like a book that needed to be opened and read for information. For example, when preparing for my first interview with Larry, I didn't prepare any questions in advance. My goal was simple: I wanted him to tell me the history of the Penitentes and his own history as a member of the Brotherhood. To me, the questions were fairly straightforward and needed no preparation. Upon reflection, I realized these would be the same kind of questions that I would have taken to a book about the Penitentes that I was reading. And just as I would expect the book to reveal and explain to

[5] The inspiration for this title comes from Robert A. Orsi "'Have You Ever Prayed to St. Jude?': Reflections on Fieldwork in Catholic Chicago," in *Reimagining Denominationalism: Interpretive Essays*, eds. Robert Bruce Mullin and Russell E. Richey (New York: Oxford University Press, 1994), 134–61. See also a revised version of the essay in Robert A. Orsi, *Between Heaven and Earth: The Religious Worlds People Make and the Scholars Who Study Them* (Princeton, NJ: Princeton University Press, 2005), 146–76.

me the details I was seeking, I was expecting Larry to behave in the same way:

> DM: I was interested in the, in the introduction [the one he gave to all assembled before the Encuentro] you'd mentioned that um [. . .] the rites that are, many rites, are celebrated these days by the penitents and the community, ah, I wasn't sure where they're from. I mean are [. . .] they're originally from Spain?

> Larry: Some of them are. We have at least, in the new book I put out, ah, we have at least twelve dominant that were catalogued as having come here from Spain and or Mexico.[6]

This is how I had initially understood ethnographic research: take the questions that you would normally pose to a book—in this case about a set of practices—but instead pose them to the person or the group of people who perform them.

I knew that there were limits to what he could say about what they did. And I kept looking for ways to get at that private information, because I knew few researchers had gotten that far. At times, however, I did wonder, "What will I do if I learn the secrets of the Penitentes?" What would I do with that information? Could I publish it? To be honest, I wasn't sure what kind of information I was seeking. In between my research visits to Seco I began researching the histories of the region—in order to get a fuller picture—and to come up with more specific questions that I could ask people when I returned. The whole goal was about getting data, especially data that couldn't be found in libraries or other research studies.

I learned much about the site and its setting from Larry in this stage of my research. He was helpful in filling in the blanks about Seco and the Hermanos there. I also followed Larry around town and listened to many of the conversations that he had with colleagues and people who listened to or read his commentaries on New Mexican life and culture.

Up until that point, my research project had called for interviewing a small number of Penitentes and other people who participated in Penitente activities. As I drew closer to recruiting volunteers, Larry suggested that I talk with the Hermano Mayor of the Brotherhood (the

[6] Larry T. Torres, interview by author, tape recording, Arroyo Seco, NM, April 2, 1999.

Head Brother) about permission to interview the members. He suspected that most of the members would be more likely to talk about their experiences if they knew I had the explicit approval of the Mesa. I spoke with the Hermano Mayor about my project and he requested that I send him all of my documentation. He would take my request before the Mesa. After the meeting date had passed, I contacted him again, but got no response. After several unsuccessful attempts at getting a response, I decided to rethink my approach. I didn't want to interview Hermanos if that meant their relationship with the Hermandad could be jeopardized.

At the same time that all this was occurring, I was undergoing a significant life transition. After two of years of talking with the leadership of my religious community over issues of celibacy and church teaching, I was removed from Roman Catholic ministry. I feared that this change in church status had the potential to derail my entire research project. If the Penitentes had any reluctance to speak with an institutional priest about what they did, how much less might they be willing to speak to a former priest. In fact, I pondered to what extent I would need to share this new information with the people. Although I said regularly that I was there as a researcher, the people knew me initially as a priest. None of the information I gathered was obtained while in a priestly role, yet I was self-conscious about my ambiguous position.

Since I decided to focus my attention on the experiences of Larry Torres and since he continued to be a willing participant in my work, I decided that if the project was going to move forward with any kind of authenticity, I would need to tell him about the developments in my life. And I did. I shared with Larry the difficulties I and other members of my community were having with the institutional church and why we felt compelled to stay, despite the pain we felt. I shared with him about the double life that priests can develop and my decision to initiate a conversation with the leadership of my community about these hard realities. As we sat there at the kitchen table, eating our breakfast, I also told him about my departure from Roman Catholic ministry. I was nervous about having this conversation with Larry but I felt like I had little choice if I wanted the research to continue. I couldn't tell him that I was no longer active in the Roman Catholic ministry without some explanation. And the whole point of my discussion with my religious community was about becoming more transparent as a priest. I was asking Larry to become transparent with me about the intimate details of his spiritual life. How could I expect him to do so if I weren't willing to do the same? The irony of the tension did not escape me.

I decided I needed to take the risk. Without my own commitment to transparency, the research wouldn't be able to continue. And without the details of the conversation, I would be betraying the call I felt as a priest to be more transparent within the Roman Catholic community. That conversation in September of 2002 changed the whole dynamic of my relationship with Larry and the quality of my research with him. My willingness to entrust him with my story, my journey of trying to move into wholeness, became a catalyst for him to become more transparent with me. The most immediate sign of this movement was that after breakfast, he got up from the table and showed me where he kept the Penitente archives in his house. He pulled out files, books, records, and pictures for me to review. He also gave me copies of the books he had written.

During the ten days that I spent with Larry at his home in Seco, Larry opened up more than the archives. He began to talk about his experiences of growing up in the Taos valley, joining the Penitentes at a young age, studying Russian language and culture in Leningrad, returning to Taos Valley and becoming a teacher. For more than a week he took me around Seco and the surrounding areas to show me some of the historical sites: the Mabel Dodge Luhan House, the Picuris Pueblo, and many other historic places, as well as art studios.

Larry also invited me back for Las Posadas (The Lodgings), which is performed for nine nights in December. So I decided to return that December for Las Posadas. A popular practice among many Hispanic communities, this tradition reenacts the story of Mary and Joseph seeking a place to lodge on their way to Bethlehem. The parishioners gather at different homes in the valley each of these nights and reenact Mary and Joseph's story, recite prayers, and join together in a feast of seasonal foods, especially posole (pork stew) and bischochitos (cookies). Larry and his family are the main organizers of this practice in the villages around Seco. They recruit a family to host Las Posadas each night. They bring the costumes and the baby doll for those who will play the roles of Mary and Joseph. Larry also brings the booklet they use for the services, which he prepared and copied.

The final evening of Las Posadas, which is often the largest gathering, is celebrated at Larry's home. He can host as many as a hundred people for the final night of Las Posadas.[7] In other communities, the ninth night is often celebrated on December 24 at the parish church. In Seco, however, the last night is typically the twenty-third, because they have an earlier Mass on Christmas Eve in the church.

In September 2002, as Larry began to speak more openly about his own life and personal experiences, I asked him if he would be willing to tell me stories from his spiritual life. He had done interviews before, but he hadn't shared so much and so deeply about his own spiritual life, especially with a researcher. We agreed on a schedule to do the sessions during my visit in December.

After doing some research about the methods of collecting life stories and life histories, I decided to begin the first session by offering Larry the opportunity to break down his life into sections. I handed him paper and pen and suggested that he create the sections according to time periods, themes, or whatever categories he wished. I didn't begin the process this way because I suspected that Larry needed any assistance in talking about his life; I was hoping that the exercise would offer me some insight into how he viewed his life. Larry didn't do the exercise. He said he didn't need it. I turned the tape recorder on and he began to speak before I even asked a question. Over the course of several days, we recorded approximately eight hours of Larry speaking about his childhood, his family, his deceased brother, the Penitentes, his being a teacher, his students, his artwork, his dreams, and the home that he built. Most of the time I listened quietly to him talk and followed along. I rarely asked a question or even made remarks. I usually just nodded along to let him know that I was listening. Those hours together were punctuated by moments of laughter, tears, and reflective silence. Most of the stories were recorded at his dinner table, located on the western end of the spacious living room in his home. At one point in the middle of the interview, he asked me what I wanted him to talk about. It was the only time that he asked me for a prompt. I suggested that he talk about his artwork. With that he

[7] The year that I attended Las Posadas, Larry invited grade school children to dance Los Matachines. Each Advent season he goes to a local grade school in the valley and teaches one group of students how to perform the dance. This particular year, he invited the children to perform the dance on his lawn after they had finished their prayers. Even if weather conditions had prevented an outdoor performance, the living room in Larry's house was large enough to handle the dance and the other guests.

began an oral tour of his home, which he had designed himself and built with the assistance of his family, friends, and students.

IN HIS OWN WORDS

What follows in this section is a selection of passages from the spiritual life stories that Larry recorded with me.[8] Due to the limitations of space, I won't include the entire collection of life stories. See appendix 3 for a fuller version of the spiritual life stories that I recorded with Larry. I have included here all the passages that deal directly with his experiences of being a Penitente and other passages where I think his comments shed light on how Larry connected being a Penitente with other aspects of his life.

In my years of researching the Penitentes in Arroyo Seco, I have experienced Larry in a number of settings. I have heard him give lectures, teach classes, and host radio programs on New Mexican culture. I have observed him teaching grade school children how to dance Los Matachines. I have watched him conduct prayer services, take the lead role in Penitente performances, and give reflections on Penitente history. I have also seen him do his performance of Archbishop Lamy, in a production sponsored by the National Endowment for the Humanities.

Larry is a performance artist. In fact, several times he acknowledged to me that he is more comfortable putting forth the ideas of someone else than he is his own. Some of the material that was presented in his life stories is similar to what Larry has shared in those other contexts. For example, when Larry spoke with me about Archbishop Lamy and Padre Martínez of Taos, he used language and stories similar to what he used in his historical performances of Lamy for the National Endowment for the Humanities.

There are many other places, however, within the recording of his spiritual life stories where Larry not only told personal stories that I haven't heard him share in public, but also spoke in a different tone. During those moments his tone grew softer and his speech became slower. He would pause more often between stories, often for as long as fifteen seconds. At these moments Larry spoke not as a

---

[8] Regarding the editing of the spiritual life stories, I have used brackets to provide additional information or to indicate unclear words in the recording. I have used ellipses to indicate a slight pause or shift in his comments and ellipses in brackets to indicate where a portion of the text was edited.

commentator on New Mexican culture and religious practice, as he does in so many other fora, but as a participant. As we'll hear, Larry is less concerned with exterior events than he is with interior experiences. In fact, this was the only time where I ever heard Larry talk about his experiences of being a Penitente. For that reason, I have chosen to privilege his narrative. Nonetheless, I will supplement his comments, where necessary, with what I have learned from Larry in other contexts. In the final section of this chapter I will analyze some of the language, images, and themes of Larry's stories.

One might say that Larry grew up in the Morada, with the Penitentes. It's not something that he would recommend for children today, even though he has grown to appreciate his experience. From the very beginning there was an element of fear associated with being a member of the Brotherhood:

I was given to the service of the Morada when I was nine, my brother Ray was eight, he also joined. Later on he dropped out when he got a girlfriend . . . decided that wasn't for him. Really, we were there to replace my uncle, my godfather, and my grandfather. [. . .] I would not recommend that children be allowed into Moradas anymore unless they are past the age of twenty-one . . . but in those days I was somehow recording everything that happened. I'm glad in retrospect that I was so young because it was my nature . . . second nature to me. I grew up really having an experience as a young Penitente, which I think is unparalleled because I have been able to write about it and study it, and analyze it and things I couldn't have done if I were already twenty-one by the time I'd joined. I had lived it. I had just lived it.

I remember the first night in the Morada that we were frightened because we're told the spirits were always out because the Morada is right smack in the middle of the cemetery and we were afraid of the dead. So that there were two Hermanos, two brothers . . . who were designated Hermano Mama, "brother mother," just to take care of the kids. I had never heard that term used in any other Morada . . . but their job, because we were too young to learn, we weren't given to the master of novices, the maestro de novicias, for to teach us our prayers . . . it was the Hermano Mama who'd just take care of us, hold our hand and make sure we weren't afraid. The job of the Hermano Mama was also to take care of the kitchen. No other Penitentes were allowed in the kitchen in those days because we didn't have paper plates or cups. We had twelve cups, twelve forks, twelve spoons, twelve plates, and we fed only twelve people at a time. Since that time now, and the invention of plastic and paper products, we feed thousands, not thousands, excuse me, hundreds of people, scores of people, and they all eat at the same time. It's changed a whole bunch in the . . . forty . . . years that I've been in it. But I remember those days, not as happy days, but as days that were necessary for my own spiritual growth. In my heart, maybe, I have always been some kind of a priest. I never took vows of anything, except to myself. But the Penitente brotherhood had probably much more of an influence on me than [. . .] than I might imagine. [Brief pause.]

Larry used the passive voice to describe his entry into the Brotherhood: He "was given to the service of the Morada." Unlike his brother, who *decided* to drop out, the Penitente life was Larry's "nature" or at least his "second nature." No one is credited with "giving" Larry to the Morada. In an interview with his mother, she explained that Larry wanted to become an Hermano.[9] Note later in this transcript how Larry will describe a friend who "*decided* to become a priest" and who "went to [. . .] seminary and [. . .] *was made* a priest" (emphasis added). Larry, too, described himself as "some kind of a priest."

Larry singled out Tinieblas (Tenebrae), from Good Friday as his favorite Penitente practice. Besides the Penitentes, the only other participants present were those who were specifically invited by them. When sharing his most detailed description of practicing Penitentismo, or Penitente Spirituality, Larry began by relating counsel he had received from Georgia O'Keeffe with his experience of Tinieblas:[10]

I learned to love the dark . . . and learned to love that which scares everybody else and as the late [Georgia] O'Keeffe once said to me ah . . . "Learn to see beauty where others can't see it. Forget the obvious beauty, where's the harsh beauty, the brutal beauty, the . . . beauty that demands" . . . and that's what I think Penitentismo is about in a large measure. Finding the solace and the beauty of death, maybe, of dealing with fear. If you've ever been in a Morada on Good

---

9 Irene Torres, interview by author, tape recording, Arroyo Seco, NM, December 16, 2002.

10 For more details about Larry's experiences with Georgia O'Keeffe, Mabel Dodge, and Dorothy Brett, see Lois Palken Rudnick, *Utopian Vistas: The Mabel Dodge Luhan House and the American Counterculture* (Albuquerque: University of New Mexico Press, 1996), 332–41, in which Rudnick concludes her book with a transcription of her interview with Larry.

Friday, when the ceremony of Tinieblas is being presented, it's one of the most wonderful things you can imagine. As the lights are being doused one at a time and we pray for the souls of widows and orphans and people who are jailed or imprisoned, people who have the most terrible will toward us at that moment in time, there's a sense of forgiveness that comes over you, that brings such peace. It's like you're to . . . letting to go not only the hurts brought in from the outside but the hurts . . . brought in from the inside and the hurts you have sent out to everybody else. Maybe not even visible hurts maybe . . . a bad thought you may have had about somebody . . . any you learn to tolerate, or either to accept . . . and suddenly the light of Christ dies out, the *lumen Christi* dies out. The last candle is extinguished and you hear the mourning of the dead as they try to break in. You hear the clanking of the chains, the rattling of the chains. You're all alone in that little room . . . maybe a few people scattered there watching you . . . in the dark and the eyes of the saints are glowing on the altar and for about fifteen minutes you are in limbo, in a very real sense, you're suspended somewhere between heaven and hell. It's not a place of suffering. It is not a purgatory. It's not a place of purging. But it is a place of coming to terms with your . . . reality. It's like being alive in your own tomb, but not trapped because knowing in a few minutes the light will come back.

It's a very pagan ritual. It's almost a fertility ritual. And it is something that I doubt very few people, outside of monks or some few select people in Rome maybe have done, have ever experienced it. It is not a seminary where you just go and read intellectually about theology and try to understand it and preach it. There's a way of feeling it at the very gut level. To be lain on a . . . packed earth floor, on your belly, with no shirt on, feeling the dampness of the earth, smelling it right next to your nostrils, and realizing that that is part of what you are is that very dirt. That you are that dirt. And maybe being whipped a couple of times and trying not to react or not to feel the sting of it . . . is . . . beyond description. It is something that is interior. You can talk about the sensations that you're going through but really, mentally, to feel your own teeth pressed against that soil, as if you were dead, as they pray for your dead brother, your dead family, or whomever and realizing you have joined them somehow physically . . . and mystically . . . is an experience that . . . you couldn't translate to a bunch of students at a university class or a high school class. And to know that it happens every year for forty years, at least at this point . . . wow . . . wow . . . that's true humbling of self because regardless of your social status or however intelligent you might think you are, it doesn't matter anymore at that point in history; you are just bone and dirt,

you're bones and dust. It is a living death . . . from which there is resurrection. And of course, fifteen minutes later when the light of Christ
comes back in and they throw open the doors and all the dead are no
longer there, there's nothing but the moon shining down upon you
and . . . there's that silence . . . maybe a cricket in the background but
. . . silence . . . and nobody says anything. You just kind of shuffle
out of the room and realize that regardless of the seasons, regardless
of the tides, regardless of your bank job or your school teaching job, at
that moment you are starting life all over again. Something that I have
never even felt even from the ecstasies of Communion, never as strong
as when I am lying on the earth floor . . . I know the priest would
not like for me to say that or to hear of it but that's the truth. That's
my truth at this moment . . . That's my truth . . . I enjoy directing all
those passion plays because it has taught me that . . . nothing is eternal and that all of these folk plays that we do, regardless of the season
of the year because they are cyclical plays . . . I find them much more
than sacred drama. I find that they are attempts to come to terms with
self as a society . . . or maybe, as just the writer, because we really
don't know who put them together in the first place. But, uh . . . but
somebody had a longing, a yearning and someway you are connecting
to that yearning and possibly not even coming up with the answer to
that yearning, but . . . experiencing that yearning to know . . . just the
need to know. Not necessarily to be used for any purpose . . . just to
know, to be, to heal, to be complete, or to be more complete if not fully
complete. [Nine-second pause.]

In this passage Larry described both the details of Penitente practice
and his experience of them from within. For him, the primary experience of Tinieblas is internal. Lying bare-chested on the Morada floor,
feeling one's teeth pressed against the dirt floor, praying for others,
and being whipped are the exterior details of the practice. On the
interior, however, something happens to the self. He recognizes that
he is also dust; he identifies his connection with those who are dead.
For him, the experience is of a "living death." This "place" that is experienced is not about suffering, purging, or purgatory. For Larry it is
about coming to terms with reality, with self. Here, all the things that
seem to matter in the day-to-day world—job, status, position—no longer have value. In fact, on this level, everyone is the same: dust, bones,
dirt. From this experience, Larry encounters "resurrection," and "starting life all over again."

Coming to terms with one's reality is an important and recurring
theme in Larry's comments:

of self . . . is probably the most important factor in
ith . . . my own, at least my own personal happiness.
come to realize that even though other people see the world
ty different from what I might see it, I will never compromise
y trying to change them to my way looking at things, to my way
ng, to my way of expressing. I usually wait for people to tell me
o they are, what they are, if they want to. And if they don't that's
fine too, but it's not up to me to say you are this, or to tell somebody
he is that or she is that. I think that is a . . . wrong. [Fourteen-second
pause; all one hears is the creaking of the wooden chairs.]

Larry doesn't force what he has learned about reality or the self onto
others. Although his Penitente experience has helped him to see that
we are all dust, bones, and dirt, he doesn't impose that onto others.
Others must come to terms with reality through their own experiences. Reality, the real self, is something we must experience on our
own. Someone else can't just tell us about it.

To say that we are dust and bones is not a matter of suggesting that
human beings are not important or valuable. Larry suggests that the
ability to see the truth about ourselves and reality is what frees us to
let go of other ways of seeing ourselves that prevent us from contribut-
ing to the world. Realizing that we are dust is what helps us transcend
the mundane world of eating, sleeping, and working:

I think, I think the big, the biggest tragedy . . . of most men . . . and I
use that in the generic sense . . . is the fact that they are not aware of
their immediate place in history. I think we all have a place in history
and roles to play, but I think when we talk about the great, what do
you call that, the . . . the quiet desperation that men are supposed to
be leading . . . the desperation doesn't stem from nonaccomplishment;
I think it stems more from the idea that they don't recognize their own
importance in history and I am not saying that they have to go out
and do great battle or design great buildings or build a fantastic statue
or build great art, just so you be consciously aware of your place in
history. Most people are not. They get up. They go to work. They eat.
They sleep. And then they die [pause]. And I think there is something
that transcends all this physicality.

Larry also acknowledged his deep desire to be seen as "different":

And a, the idea or the perception that there is a need to be special or
different in some way and you don't know why, you just know you

80

have to or die trying . . . was something made abundantly clear to me. The idea of not being recognized as something different . . . on my terms . . . [DM: uh um] on my terms is abhorrent to me.

Larry also explored more deeply this perspective on being "special" or "different," how that relates to his sense of self, and his relationship with society. How he perceived himself and what he did with that perception are what Larry expects he will consider at the end of his life:

> I remember a priest asked me once if I believed in God . . . and he was kind of shocked when I said I believe that there is a God . . . for those who need a God. Something that takes you a little while to realize . . . So the question is "Do you need a God?" . . . Now that is harder to answer than "Is there a God? Do you believe in God?" [DM: Was he asking you?] Uh-huh. [DM: Do you need a God?] No. He didn't ask me. He didn't think that far. He just sat there stunned beyond belief. [I laughed.] I asked myself do I need a God. And the answer was . . . I probably do, even if it is only the God within me. I think it is important to recognize the divine in oneself . . . Modestly and full of pride at the same time . . . Because I really think that creation, creativity is a gift and . . . I'd like to think when I am doing is that I am reliving the tale of the ten talents—in particular taking talent very literally, but I think that for some reason we do have certain gifts, different gifts, just like every flower out in there in meadow has different petals and different sizes, different sets of roots. And all of them are their different root to the beauty to the harmony of the entire thing . . . if we do their job correctly. And if we are too afraid to move or to express . . . we might as well never have lived. I think the question I am going to ask myself toward the end of my life is more a question of . . . "Did I do what I needed, not only for myself, but for everybody else?" Not, "Did I go to church?" Not, "Did I own a car?" "Did I live in a castle?" Was, "Did I bother to . . . reach out to somebody, in some way? Did it make me a better person? Did that help *them* in some way?" These aren't just Christian ideals; these are fundamental universal truths that need to be spoken and expressed to everybody else. And it doesn't matter what the social status is we have.

This seeking of our true selves in order that we would know our place in history, in society, and therefore, be able to make our contribution to society is fundamental to being Christian and to being human, regardless of who we are. For Larry, there is no place where he can escape these questions. For him, this is what Penitentismo has taught him about the spiritual life.

That's not to say that Larry hasn't looked to others for help in how to interpret what he is experiencing in his life. Throughout his life he has turned to priests for help in this process. He expects them not only to have struggled with the same process of self-identity, but also to have arrived at a place from which they can help others in this process:

I used to have a priest friend, turned actor, the late José Rodríguez was with RADA, the Royal Academy of Dramatic Arts in London. He was a protégé of John Gielgud. One day he decided to become a priest in New Mexico and I asked him why. He had founded a Spanish theater company in New Mexico, in Albuquerque, called La Compañía de Teatro. And he had written a play called La Pasión de Jesús Chávez in which Jesus is portrayed as a Chicano who has been imprisoned and sits there telling a story that parallels and mimics the life of Christ, in the passion of Christ. One day he was asked to perform this for the peregrinos, the young men and women who walk to Chimayó at the beginning of the summer every year from all four directions of the compass and combine . . . and a . . . come together at the Santuario— seven days later. Well he happened to perform this and in a very real sense he became the Cristo to these young men who were listening to him that night. As he told me that night, he said, . . . "I had performed on many stages but I didn't know that night was to change my life, cause suddenly I finished and there was absolute silence. Then everybody stood up off that gym floor and said (yelling) 'Cristo! Cristo! Cristo!'" And they threw him into the air. He said they kept throwing him into the air. "I was the Cristo in a very real sense to me," he said. "That was my moment of conversion, like St. Paul being hit by a lightning bolt. Suddenly I realized that I could do much better on the altar if I use my theatrical arts for homiletics instead." And he went to Mount Angel Seminary and he . . . was made priest. And it was to change his life. When we were very good friends he was sent to Arroyo Seco, where we kept him in the summer and he . . . helped us found our own theater company, La Santísima Trinidad, of which I became the first director. [. . .] I remember the night he was to be ordained, the night before he was to be ordained, we're sitting around talking in Seco and he said, oh yeah, he said, "Tomorrow I become a prince of the church." He said, "My head will be put on a pi . . . a silken cushion." And I laughed, and he narrowed his vision, which always meant that he meant business. He said, "What do you want?" And I said, "The church of New Mexico already has too many kings and queens, and princes." He said, "What do you want from me?" I said, "Instead of seeing your face on a silken cushion tomorrow, I want to see it in the dust." He took a deep breath, and h-he said, "You're on, bro. You're on. You bring it." The following morning, on the way to the cathedral of Santa Fe, my parents and I stopped at the . . . holy chapel of Chimayó and picked up the dirt from the Papu [called El Posito in Chimayó], the little hole where the holy dirt is. We wrapped it in a purificator and I told Fr. Conran [Runnebaum] who was co-officiating that day that this was to be put under his chin at the moment of consecration. Sure enough, he was brought in . . . the . . . up the nave, laid in cruciform in front of the cathedral and just as his chin was to be put on a silken cushion, I had it whisked away and motioned for Fr. Conran to open the purificator. He opened the purificator and there was the holy dirt of Chimayó and he . . . his chin rested on it. And he turned and he looked at me. I told him that if he was to serve the people of New Mexico, I wanted to see his face in the dust at the moment of his highest glory. [. . .] Well, he became the priest of Abiquiu, which was the birthplace of the great Padre Martínez of Taos. And he was to serve there for six years and practice humility, which is not easy for him, no easier for him than it would be for me.

Whether a priest or not, the spiritual life is not about seeking social status or power, according to Larry. "I want to see it [his face] in the dust," is the *practice* Larry prescribed for his friend. Seeing oneself as a "prince of the church" was a distraction. Based on Larry's experience, identifying with the dust of the earth is how one discovers oneself and one's place within society.

As we heard above, intelligence and education, including seminary education, can't replace what can only be learned through experience, spiritual practices, and reflection. Larry respects intelligence. But it's not enough for him. Larry has expected the priests in his life to know this. He is, however, often disappointed:

I'm a . . . in the middle of a struggle with one of our local priests . . . and a . . . what's interesting about this case is that . . . I see in the man . . . the antithesis of everything else that I thought I was. I don't hate him. I kind of admire him actually, because he's intellectual. But what is interesting is that I've come to realize that just, the sheer intelligence means nothing by itself if it is intolerant . . . I think . . . it is important to be able to reach as many people as possible, really I think that is the reason we are on this earth . . . is to reach. I don't think in the end if there is something called a judgment that we are going to be judged how many times we went to Mass or how many times we didn't. I think it is important . . . to . . . reach, or maybe to love . . .

and I'm not again speaking of just a sexual relationship; I am speaking of the idea to open up yourself to as many different ideas, to allow yourself to be vulnerable on occasion and to give others or to afford others the opportunity to be vulnerable in your presence without any kind of judgment . . . and my heart bleeds when I see people who remind me of me at a certain stage in my life where I just couldn't be open to anybody . . . and so how do you reach out to somebody, sometimes you do it by condemning maybe, maybe by telling them that what they are doing is wrong or stupid, a tradition, a cultural is for the weak-minded.

Becoming vulnerable, seeing oneself as dust, admitting one's limitations, has implications beyond self-discovery. There are communal dimensions to the practice of allowing others to see our vulnerability; we allow others to identify and embrace their own vulnerability. For Larry, the vulnerability of the priest is not simply a matter of good modeling for others, or the development of his spiritual life. The spiritual life of the community is at issue.

One way Larry has sought to address this issue of vulnerability within his community has been to provide children with a practice to help them deal with their fears. Utilizing his own experience and his training as a teacher Larry has self-published a coloring book that is used in the local grade schools. The original sketches line the walls of the guest room in his home:

And on the final wall, right over the bed is the whole story of fear in northern New Mexico that is called Cocas y Coconas, or the Bogey Creatures of the Hispanic Southwest. I went to forty-two or forty-seven different villages and I asked them for, to tell me what the face of fear was in their village and to help me draw it and I would draw it and they'd say, "No, no, not like this—like this." Or, "Yeah, yeah—you're doing fine." And they would identify it for me. I thought it was very important in the history of New Mexico to unmask the bogeyman because so long as you do not unmask the bogeyman, he tends to have power over you. But if you can identify what the bogeyman does or what it represents then there is no longer reason to fear. So I re-created this children's book on the Spanish monsters of the Southwest and gave it to various elementary schools so the kids can study it, color it, tear it apart, and it hath no domain over them, as it were.

Just as Penitentismo has shaped Larry's inner world and his spiritual journey, drawing, painting, and performing have been significant ways in which Larry has sought to depict how he has experienced this inner world and what it means to him. Every room of his home is full of his artwork—depictions of Penitentismo and New Mexican culture and the world they created within him:

> We'll talk about the steps leading toward the bedroom. You see six huge canvas pieces that are up there. The one closest to the bedroom door, shows me lying in my bed, surrounded by all my nightmares, all the things that go bump in the night. It was important that these things be painted; that they be researched, not only because they are part of the patrimony of fear that we had, but also because of the painting I was able to let go of a lot of hurts and a lot of pa . . . a lot of my childhood. I hardly look at them anymore, because they have su . . . become such an integral part of what I am. Somebody once said, "Boy, you must have a great imagination to have created all these." The answer was, even if I could, I wo . . . I couldn't have done it myself. I am not that talented. I am not that . . . that . . . that gifted to have created all these things. These are created by the culture. All I do is record what was created by the culture.

> Right next to that there is another huge piece which has my coffin and my coffin . . . on my coffin I inscribed the words "era y soy polvo." "I was and I am dust." I thought it was a wonderful thing to put on my coffin and it . . . there are seven different grotesque figures. Of course, the biggest is San. Sebastiana herself; she is lady death. And then she is followed by . . . on one side, she is flanked on the left by the lady of the ax. That is another aspect of death. And then on the other side . . . is the . . . lady who's carrying, "what was it?" The lady of the ax . . . then there's a horrifying death next to her and then there is a prodigious death next to her; there's the joyful death next to her. There are a couple of ones that I can't remember but it shows you that Spanish do not take death for granted. The idea that there are seven different forms of death because death is not just death is not just death. How you die is just as important as how you live. And so . . . sometimes death can be very tragic, sometimes it can be faminous, sometimes it can be absolutely beautiful—like at the end of a long happy life, where you have made peace and it's just time to let go.

Through his experience of being a Penitente for over forty years, Larry came to know that he was and is dust. Similar to the children with their coloring books, Larry has used his painting as a way to face this reality. Painting a picture of his coffin with "era y soy polvo" on it suggests that he has come to terms with this reality. In fact, his depiction of the "seven different" kinds of death suggests that he is no longer worried about how he will die. Although Larry didn't articulate it in words, his painting communicates that even the Spanish stratification of death and the fear that it propagates have lost their power over him.

PENITENTE PRACTICES AS A WAY OF KNOWING

If we were to speculate about why Larry is reticent to speak more publicly about his experiences we may think it is due to the laws that the church prescribes for the Brotherhood. That may be partly true. Larry's comments, however, indicate that there is a more compelling reason to be slow to speak about these practices. These practices are a way of knowing for Larry. They are a way to know the self, death, and resurrection. And to one who is not a participant, who has not been initiated into these practices, understanding would be limited, if not impossible. In fact, Larry makes a point to contrast this way of knowing with the kind of knowing that happens in a classroom. More specifically, he contrasts it with what happens in theology classes in seminaries. People who study Christian theology, including most priests and members of religious communities don't know what Larry knows, because they don't practice what he practices. In fact, they don't even know that they don't know.

Larry claims that Penitente spirituality or Penitentismo, as he calls it, addresses his need to know. He wants to know himself, as in, he wants to better understand himself. But he also wants to know new life, as in, he wants to have an experience of new life. That is what the practices of penance provide for Larry. In pushing himself to know his limits, he is given the chance to detach, to lose control, to lose himself. The paradox is that it is in this loss that he experiences life anew. This fits into the larger theme of making the hidden known, which is prevalent in these comments and in his artwork. Experiencing, expressing, and reflecting are all ways in which Larry seeks to know what is hidden, in him, and in the world.

Lying on the Earth Floor

Dust is everywhere in New Mexico, especially in Arroyo Seco. Many of the roads are dirt roads. Most of the houses, the churches, the Moradas, and the stores are adobe (mud) structures. The dry, windy climate means that dust is often swirling all around. Dust is a regular part of life. Keeping one's clothes, boots, and vehicles free from mud and dust is an impossible task.

The Morada in Seco is almost completely made of dirt. It is a traditional adobe structure with thick mud walls and dirt floors. While lying on the dirt floor of the Morada, praying for the dead and for others, and being whipped by a Brother, Larry realizes that he is like most everything around him: dust. He was dust and he is dust. This is central to Larry's experience of Penitente spirituality. "Era y soy polvo," is similar to the words used with the imposition of ashes on Ash Wednesday in Roman Catholic churches and increasingly in some Protestant churches: "Remember, you are dust, and to dust you will return." One striking difference between the two phrases is that Larry's version lacks the projection into the future. There is no, "I will be dust," or "I will return to dust."

Larry's realization is starker. There is no point at which he is more than dust. This is his reality. Nothing can change this. Not the seasons. Not the movements of the oceans. Not one's intelligence. Not one's social position. Each year on Good Friday, Larry comes face-to-face with this realization, which allows him to let go of everything. This is the new life that he seeks to know. Here, he experiences healing.

It's worth noting that even though Larry's insight into life as dust echoes the message of Ash Wednesday, Larry doesn't identify that connection or make that comparison. Larry compares this experience to that of the "ecstasies of Communion." His experiences of lying on the earth floor speak more to him than his experiences of receiving Communion. Communion with the dust of the earth allows him to connect with the "yearning [. . .] to be complete, or to be more complete if not fully complete."

Priests and Princes

As the narrative above indicates, Larry's relationships with priests often, but not always, include tensions around spirituality. Most of the priests who have served in Arroyo Seco have not been members of the Hermandad. During my research, I heard about only one priest who had been an active member, many years ago, in the Morada in Seco. Larry's comments suggest that even when the priests are educated, intelligent, and dedicated, they do not understand the spiritual practices of the Brotherhood. On the one hand, Larry doesn't expect them to understand Penitente practices when they first arrive. One can't understand them by reading books. On the other hand, Larry does expect the priests to seek to understand what the Brothers do and what it means for them.

Larry's concerns, however, go deeper than a desire for the priests to appreciate Penitente spiritual practices. He assumes that the struggle of coming to terms with oneself and with reality is the spiritual task of both priests and laypeople alike. The practices that one uses to engage that task may differ, but the struggle is the same. He expects the priests of the church to be active in that spiritual struggle, to be aware of its marks, and to accompany others in the process. In short, Larry expects to find in the priest another person who seeks to know the truth about himself and who is able to help others in their search.

With the case of his friend José, Larry was concerned with his friend's potential attachment to the social status he would achieve by becoming a priest. In response, Larry didn't counter with another vision of priesthood; he prescribed a practice: put your face in the dust. Practices, not intellectual arguments, are where Larry puts his trust. Based on his experience, spiritual practices help one let go of exterior things, such as social status, in order to encounter the interior world. Larry believed that José's attachment to becoming "a prince of the church" would have distracted him from coming to terms with himself, and it would have prevented him from discovering who he was in relationship to the community.

DO YOU NEED GOD?

I began this chapter by quoting part of a discussion Larry once had with a priest. Larry didn't provide the context. He simply shared what happened when a priest one day asked him if he believed in God. For Larry, that isn't the real question. For him, the real question is "Do you need a God?" Larry took the priest's question about faith in God and turned it into the question "Do we need God?" For Larry, how one struggles with and answers this question would reveal a lot more about a person. The priest, however, according to Larry, "didn't go that far."

From an early age, Larry learned to love the dark, to love the things that inspired fear in other people. As he described his experience of growing up within the Brotherhood, we get the sense that the Penitente practices both inspired fear in him and helped him to face his fears. Seeking to make sense of his experience, Larry invoked the advice he received from Georgia O'Keeffe about learning to see beauty where others can't. Learn to see "the harsh beauty, the brutal beauty, the . . . beauty that demands," Larry remembered O'Keeffe telling him.

O'Keeffe wasn't speaking simply about visually seeing the "harsh beauty" that is outside us. She was, most importantly, talking about being able to see the harsh beauty of ourselves.[11] Larry knew what she meant. For him, Penitentismo is about facing the harsh reality of life. He is dust. He has enemies. Those he loves will die. He needs forgiveness. He clings to social status. He thinks ill of others at times. He sometimes feels the absence of God. He has many fears. He is not perfect. He has limits. He needs God. These are some of the harsh realities that Larry has learned to see because of his practice of Penitentismo. If being a Penitente has helped Larry learn to see the harsh beauty of life and to face his fears, then his life as an artist, both in performance and in media, has helped him communicate those experiences to others.

Larry's spiritual life stories don't provide us with many details about Penitente practices that scholars don't already know, but he has shared with us how he experiences those practices, how they have shaped his life, and how they have helped him come to terms with his self. Penitente practices are his way of coming to self-knowledge.

[11] For a detailed discussion of O'Keeffe's perspectives on painting, beauty, and the self, see Susan Krieger, *Social Science and the Self: Personal Essays on an Art Form* (New Brunswick, NJ: Rutgers University Press, 1991), 67–84, where she writes, "The idea of striving to speak from within, to make one's particular unknown known, is different from the idea of striving to speak about something outside the self. O'Keeffe believes that the mountains she paints exist in the desert landscape aside from her, but when she paints, she grasps not for those external mountains, but for her view of them, and the difference between the two kinds of efforts is important."

Chapter 4

Ethnography as Theology

INTRODUCTORY REMARKS

In this chapter we return to the two conversations that I introduced in the introduction. The first conversation is about the contribution that ethnographic research can make to theological studies. The second is about the practices of Los Hermanos Penitentes in Arroyo Seco, what they do and how they interpret those practices within their context. We'll begin with the latter conversation because it will provide us with a concrete, specific illustration of how ethnographic research can be a powerful way to reflect with other Christians, engaging them in dialogue about their spiritual practices, their everyday lives, and the ways in which they interpret those experiences. In the end, we'll see that ethnographic research can go beyond gathering data and learning to see others more clearly. Ethnographic research can also be an act of primary theology. It can become a form of prayerful beholding and attentiveness.

Persistent Questions in Penitente Studies

The exact origins of the La Fraternidad Piadosa de Nuestro Padre Jesús Nazareno are not known. Nonetheless, commentators have postulated different theories about how the Brotherhood emerged in the Southwest United States. Although these theories have differed significantly, they have been divided into two categories: the "indigenous development" theories and the "late transplant" theories.[1] As Michael P. Carroll points out in *The Penitente Brotherhood*, the theories

---

[1] Michael P. Carroll, *The Penitente Brotherhood: Patriarchy and Hispano-Catholicism in New Mexico* (Baltimore, MD: Johns Hopkins University Press, 2002), 27–30. See also William Wroth, *Images of Penance, Images of Mercy: Southwestern Santos in the Late Nineteenth Century* (Norman: University of Oklahoma Press, 1991), 42–47, for an earlier, slightly different categorization.

proposing an "indigenous development" postulate that the Brotherhood emerged as a result of the training and example of the Franciscan friars who were part of the early European settlers. In these theories, the Penitente Brotherhood emerged as a local version of the Franciscan Third Order. In chapter 1 we discussed how Archbishop Salpointe, in the late nineteenth century, made a point of establishing the emergence of Penitente practices and the Hermandad within the development of the Franciscan Third Order in New Mexico. The "late transplant" category includes a number of theories about how the Brotherhood developed sometime in the first years of the nineteenth century and was modeled after confraternities (cofradías) found in Spain and Mexico at that time. In this category, Carroll puts the perspectives of Angélico Chávez, Thomas Steele, and William Wroth.

Recent scholarship on the Penitentes continues to be skeptical about the Brotherhood having its roots in the practices of the Franciscan Third Order. In *The Penitente Brotherhood* Carroll, a professor of sociology from the University of Western Ontario, argues that the "indigenous development" theory relies on assumptions about the Spanish community of the eighteenth century that are unfounded. We'll return to his work later in this chapter. In *The Sacred World of the Penitentes* Alberto López Pulido, a professor of American Studies at Arizona State University West, argues that the claim of association between the Franciscan Third Order and the Hermandad was a narrative generated by the Roman Catholic Church, particularly propounded by Jesuit missionaries in Las Vegas, New Mexico, Archbishop Lamy, and Archbishop Salpointe, in order to gain control over the Brotherhood and to silence them.[2] Pulido contends that these church authorities did this by proclaiming that the Brotherhood was a remnant of the Franciscan Third Order that had spun out of control and needed to reclaim its earlier obedience to the authority of the church (read: archbishop).

In the account of the feast day of Nuestra Señora de los Dolores in the first appendix of this book, I noticed in Larry's explanation to the people gathered that night in Arroyo Hondo that the Franciscans were responsible for organizing and cultivating the Penitente Brotherhood in New Mexico. This is not an unusual statement by Larry. I heard him make it numerous times over the course of my research. I heard him make this point on a Good Friday when speaking about the events of

[2] Alberto López Pulido, *The Sacred World of the Penitentes* (Washington, DC: Smithsonian Institution Press, 2000), 38–59.

the day to those gathered. I heard him tell the peregrinos (pilgrims) the same thing as we gathered for the first night of Las Posadas and shivered in the cold night air. I also saw this explanation in the outline notes and overhead transparencies he uses when teaching the Penitentes about their history.

At first glance, we might assume that Larry's comments about the Franciscan roots of the Brotherhood indicate that his perspective neatly coincides with the "indigenous development" theory described above. Larry is aware of the different hypotheses about the origins of the Brotherhood. Having been a Penitente for over forty years and serving as the archivist of the Seco Morada, it would make sense that he would have an opinion on this topic. Larry is also well aware of the Brotherhood's history of suppression by the church. We have seen that throughout his comments. Why then, would he continue to advocate continuity between these two entities, especially if it was originally suggested as a way for church leadership to control and possibly eradicate the activities of the Brotherhood?

That question can be answered by taking a closer look at Larry's comments. In his remarks at the feast day celebration, we hear that Larry not only puts Penitente practices in continuity with the Franciscan tradition, but also with the larger Christian ascetic tradition, going all the way back to Anthony of the desert.[3] On two other occasions I heard him include Anthony, St. Benedict, and St. Francis in his accounts. This is similar to the narrative he uses when teaching other Penitentes about their history. Larry's placement of the Penitente practices within the larger context of the ascetical tradition within Christianity modifies the claim of Franciscan connections. The modifications made in his account reframe the "indigenous development" narrative in two important ways.

First, by expanding the narrative to include Anthony of the desert and St. Benedict, Larry is proposing that the connection between the Penitentes and these early figures in Christian history is one of similarity of approaches to the Christian life. The connection is not one of direct descent. To put it more simply, the intentions of the Penitentes are parallel to other ascetic practices in the Christian tradition: to come

[3] Anthony was a Christian monk of the fourth century. Although being born into a wealthy family, he decided to sell all his possessions and to practice asceticism after hearing the words of the Gospel of Matthew. After a period of living in solitude with another monk, then living in a tomb, Anthony moved into the Egyptian desert.

to a deeper knowledge of God and oneself through strict disciplining of the body. This is not to say that Larry doesn't believe there are some direct connections between the Brotherhood and the Franciscan Order as a whole. Those connections, however, are much more complex than the Brotherhood being a remnant of the Franciscan Third Order.

The second way Larry's perspective modifies the "indigenous development" narrative is connected to the first, but more profound. By appealing to the larger ascetical tradition within the history of Christianity, Larry subverts the claims of Archbishop Lamy, Archbishop Salpointe, and anyone else for that matter, of being the sole authority or interpreter of what is appropriate as a Christian practice. The longstanding practice of Christian asceticism since the fourth century provides a precedent for the Brotherhood and their practices and it supplies them with a place of legitimacy within the Christian community.

If church authorities did establish the direct connection between the Franciscan Third Order in New Mexico and the emergence of the Brotherhood in order to gain control over Los Hermanos Penitentes and to eventually suppress its activities, their attempts failed. In fact, when we look at the way in which Larry reformulates the narrative, we can see that, to the contrary, the church authorities provided the Hermandad with a framework of legitimacy. After noticing the ambiguities in Penitente history and reflecting on the different theories, I asked Larry about my interpretation of his narrative about the emergence of the Brotherhood in relationship to the other theories, as I have just described above. When I told him that I thought that he was using the church's argument to suppress them for his own purposes of creating a legitimate space for Penitente practice, he looked at me and grinned. He didn't comment any further.

Before proceeding further, I want to note here that the way Larry shapes his narratives about the origins of the Penitente Brotherhood goes beyond modifying the narrative presented by church leaders in order to claim legitimacy for Penitente practices. He is claiming a modification in the authority structure of the church based on his experience as a Penitente. We return to that discussion later in this chapter.

PENITENTE PRACTICES AND THE SELF

By connecting Penitentismo with the tradition of asceticism in the Christian church, Larry also establishes a connection between their practices and the monastic tradition. He wants the Penitente practices to be seen in their fullest context: a way of life that assists one in coming to terms with reality, and in particular, with oneself. This is why Larry laments the fact that so many scholars, tourists, and church leaders who have visited northern New Mexico over the years have often focused almost singularly on the fact that the Brothers practice flagellation. That is to say, part of their practice includes stripping to the waist and either whipping oneself on the back or being whipped by another Penitente.[4] Traditionally, the intention behind flagellation is the expiation of sins. The sins could be those of the one being whipped, the sins of their loved ones, the sins of all humankind, or the sins of those (souls) in purgatory.[5] The suffering that one endures is meant to reduce any potential suffering in purgatory.

Flagellation remains a practice in the Morada in Arroyo Seco and at least some of the Brothers continue to interpret their practices in relationship to expiating sins. On several occasions I heard one of the elected leaders of the Morada speak about the souls in purgatory and how important it was for the Brothers to pray for them and to do acts of penance for their release.[6] Larry, however, offers us a very different interpretation of his experience. In chapter 3 we saw that Larry makes it clear that his experience of being a Penitente, including the practice of flagellation, is not a matter of suffering (entering purgatory) on account of sins committed, nor a matter of purging oneself, as a way to affect healing. Instead, it is a doorway to knowledge of the self. To help us to make further sense of Larry's description of his experience, I suggest we utilize the work of Talal Asad and Brian Mahan.

Bodily Pain and Truth

In *Genealogies of Religion: Discipline and Reasons of Power in Christianity and Islam*, Asad dedicates two chapters to the discussion of the

[4] The whip, called a disciplina, is usually made of woven fibers from the yucca plant or sisal fibers.

[5] Wroth, *Images of Penance*, 10–12. Here, Wroth describes how the practice of flagellation has been both promoted and condemned by authorities in the Roman Catholic Church.

[6] I should also note that one of the pastors of the parish, while making an announcement about a Mass to be celebrated that week in the Morada, said that offering the Mass was the most important thing they could do for the souls in purgatory. His comment makes me wonder about the extent to which there could be significant differences among clergy and Penitentes about how important flagellation is for the expiation of sins.

relationship between pain and truth within both the legal system and the church during the medieval period. Due to the limitations of space I cannot provide a comprehensive accounting of Asad's observations into the relationship between pain and truth and the different ways in which that relationship has been constructed. Instead, I simply want to outline several of his insights as a point of comparison with the way in which Larry described his experience of Penitente practices.

I am particularly interested in how Asad discusses the use of pain within the monastic tradition as a way to obtain the truth about oneself. According to Asad, "The monastic program that prescribes the performance of rites is directed at forming and reforming Christian dispositions. The most important of these is the will to obey what is seen as the truth, and, concomitantly, the guardians of that truth. The achievement of that disposition is the Christian virtue of humility."[7] In other words, through the monastic program of discipline, a monk is schooled in the disposition of obedience. That obedience comes not from destroying the monk's will, but from reshaping that will so that he wants to obey. Ultimately, the practice of obedience leads to the development of the key virtue: humility. A central part of that program of discipline was the practice of penance, which included some form of mental or physical pain as a way to produce truth from within the monk.

Asad claims that the major reason for doing penance, which was done voluntarily, was to avoid a greater punishment in purgatory. The medieval penitentials instructed the confessor/priest to remind the penitent that one had to suffer either here on earth or in purgatory for the sins that one committed. By practicing acts of penance here, one could reduce the amount of suffering one would have to do in purgatory. Pain and suffering were considered both a consequence of committing sin and the consequence of not admitting one's guilt. Not admitting one's guilt here on earth and suffering the necessary penance was seen as a denial of the truth about one's life, which just increased the amount of penance one would need to do. This is why suffering in purgatory was thought to be worse than any suffering one could do here.

In the end, however, what is significant according to Asad is not the threat of future suffering, but the way in which suffering and pain

[7] Talal Asad, *Genealogies of Religion: Discipline and Reasons of Power in Christianity and Islam* (Baltimore, MD: Johns Hopkins Press, 1993), 131.

became associated with facing the truth about one's sinfulness. Asad explains that "self punishment constitutes a crucial feature of monastic discipline in the Middle Ages and that its program was provided in the writings of the early Greek and Latin Fathers, which were regularly studied in monastic communities. The body was to be chastised, we are told, because it was an obstacle to the attainment of perfect truth."[8] Relying on Foucault's analysis of monastic programs of discipline, Asad maintains that bodily pain was an indispensable part of the program because the body was responsible for becoming attached to the urges, feelings, and sensations that can be destructive to the soul. The point here is not to learn to despise the body. The challenge is to deal with the urges of the body in light of the monk's pursuit of truth about himself. To put it another way, the body becomes the arena for discovering the truth about oneself because the body is the weakest, therefore most vulnerable aspect of being human.

Penance became known as medicine for the sinful condition of humanity. Asad explains:

> The concept of penance as medicine for the soul was no fanciful metaphor, but a mode of organizing the practice of penance in which bodily pain (or extreme discomfort) was linked with the pursuit of truth—at once literal and metaphysical. For it required of the penitent to report the truth about his relevant condition to the physician, information that was essential for the latter to diagnose the sickness properly and to prescribe for it the appropriate cure.[9]

What is important for the Christian monk to remember, Asad claims, is that the human condition is one in which the soul is always sick to some extent. Even when there are no particular sins to admit, the Christian still has the potential for sin. This is the truth that we need to face. Consequently, we are always in need of medicine, which is why the Christian needs to be attentive to the possibility that he or she may be in denial about this potentiality. The goal is not only to submit oneself to the authority of the priest and the penance prescribed, but also to punish oneself as a way to avoid the potentiality of sinning altogether.

[8] Ibid., 106.
[9] Ibid., 103–4.

Besides discovering the truth that one is sinful and always has the potential to commit sin, the ascetic also discovers one other important truth: God's grace and forgiveness. Recognition of this truth, however, can only come after one can honestly admit the truth about one's sinfulness. The truth of God's offer of forgiveness is the ultimate medicine for the Christian's sinful condition. This is what brings healing to both body and soul, even if it is only temporary.

This process of subjecting oneself to these truths was done by subjecting oneself to the authority of the priest or abbot. Asad writes, "[T]he admission of guilt by the penitent to the confessor was the recognition of the truth about oneself and at the same time the presentation of oneself as a sick soul in need of help. It was this collaborative activity that sustained the authority relationship between priest and penitent."[10] Admitting to oneself that one had sinned was not enough. The discipline demanded that one make his or her confession to the priest. In addition, one would not have access to the truth about God's grace and forgiveness if they didn't subject themselves to the priest, who is God's representative. The program of discipline, then, established and maintained the authority of the priest and the necessity of submitting oneself to it.

Resonances and Differences

If we use these points from the work of Asad as a point of comparison with what Larry has to say about his experiences of being a Penitente, it will allow us to understand Larry's comments more fully. Both describe a similar goal of humility. Their descriptions of the details of the processes of penance, however, have some interesting resonances and differences. For the sake of this discussion, I will identify and briefly explore four points of comparison: the truth that one is seeking in penance, how bodily pain is associated with truth, the role of priestly authority in penance, and what happens to the self in the process.

The first point of comparison is a very important one: the truth that one is seeking in performing penance. According to Asad, the truth is twofold for the ascetic. The first element of truth is that human beings commit sinful acts sometimes and have the potential to sin at all times. Consequently, the Christian is always in need of medicine. In this life, there is no permanent cure. The second element of truth one discovers

[10] Ibid.

in penance is the grace and mercy of God, experienced through the offer of forgiveness delivered through the priest. And just as the pain of sin affects both body and soul, so does God's grace and forgiveness reach to both. For Larry, we see a very different kind of truth emerging from his penitential experiences. Larry doesn't call it a search for "truth." He calls it "coming to terms with reality" or "mak[ing] our own . . . peace . . . with our own reality, with our own self."[11] The "reality" Larry is talking about is not that we are sinful, although he wouldn't deny that, but that we are vulnerable and fragile. We were and we are dust. In this way, we are just like those who are dead. For him, being finite is not the same as being sinful.

This "reality" that Larry describes leads us to the second point of comparison: how bodily pain is associated with discovering the truth about ourselves. According to Asad, bodily pain became associated with truth in Western monasticism of the Middle Ages because the body was considered to be a significant obstacle in the pursuit of the truth about one's spiritual condition. The weaknesses and fragilities of the body made the soul particularly vulnerable to urges, feelings, and desires. Disciplining the body to resist these urges would make the soul less vulnerable to sin. For Larry, bodily pain is also associated with the pursuit of truth. For him, however, bodily pain is a concrete expression of how vulnerable we are. Even when he "tries not to feel the sting" of a couple of whips, he is reminded of just how vulnerable he is. Here, the discipline is about submitting to one's own vulnerability, which is the reality of being human. For Larry, bodily pain is not to be associated with our being sinful or being susceptible to sinful desires, but with the vulnerability that comes from being made of dust.

These first two points of comparison between Larry's experience and the insights on medieval monasticism presented by Asad suggest that there would be differences in the way in which priestly authority is understood. These differences are significant. As we read above, the practice of penance as Asad described it assigned the priest a very critical role in the process. The necessity of confessing one's sins to the priest in order to face the truth about one's life and to receive the grace of God's forgiveness necessitated collaboration between priest and penitent. It also demanded the penitent to subject himself or herself to

[11] Larry T. Torres, interview by author, tape recording, Arroyo Seco, NM, December 14–16, 2002. All of Larry's quotations in this chapter come from this interview.

priestly authority on a regular basis, unless one was willing to suffer significantly in purgatory.

The important truth that Larry has discovered in the penitential process is that he has a vulnerable and fragile existence. That insight, however, does not require him to subject himself to priestly authority in order to receive forgiveness. There is nothing sinful about being vulnerable. In fact, according to Larry, allowing others to see that you are vulnerable is a gift that you can offer others. This is not to say that Larry does not acknowledge priestly authority. He does. After reading his comments about seminarians, priests, bishops, and even a pope in the previous chapters, we can see more clearly now how he understands the source of their authority. For him, priestly authority is intimately connected with the priest's "coming to terms" with his own human reality. The priest, the pope, and the bishop, like all Christians, must come to terms with their own vulnerability and fragility. For Larry, the priest's authority is not primarily derived from his ability to dispense God's grace, but from the priest's willingness to submit himself to the truth about his own life and existence. The priest and the penitent share the same struggle, the same path, and they both share the same reality. Both are called to a life of humility.

The last point of comparison I wish to make here concerns the way in which penitential actions affect the self. For Asad, penance is one part, probably the central one, of the larger monastic program of forming and reforming the self. The goal is to create the disposition of humility in the monk. This goal is not achieved by destroying the self or by obliterating the will of the monk. On the contrary, the objective is to shape the will of monk so that he wants to obey the rule of the monastery.

Larry also sees the disposition of humility as the desired outcome of the practice of penance. Humility arises not from recognizing that one is sinful, but from realizing that one is vulnerable. Like the monastic program, Penitentismo, according to Larry, does not entail a destruction of the self. Nor does it seem to entail a reorganizing or reformation of the self. Larry's comments indicate that the process is a matter of letting go of the self, or at least what we consider to be ourselves, for example, social status or material wealth. The way Larry experiences the invitation to let go of the self is when he has his teeth pressed against the mud floor of the Morada, he is feeling the pain of being whipped, and the Hermanos are praying for deceased members of his family. In those moments he recognizes that because he shares with the deceased in the dust of the earth, he also shares death. This is the reality of oneself. Not one's job or one's status or one's wealth. Another element of truth emerges after this moment of recognition. Just as the Christian monk experiences the truth of God's grace after telling the truth about his sinful condition, Larry experiences a new beginning. There is a resurrection. Larry and the other Hermanos return to their daily lives and the various ways in which human beings distinguish themselves from one another, but with the knowledge that what they share in common speaks more about the truth of their selves. In fact, this process goes beyond acknowledging the truth about ourselves. The truth about us as a society is also revealed. As a society we do not support the process of coming to know our true selves.

The Project of Transforming the Self

In chapter 1 we reviewed the history of the Penitentes in New Mexico, including their relationships with a number of priests, bishops, archbishops, and Pope Pius IX. When reflecting on that history, along with Larry's comments on the exchanges that have taken place between the Hermandad and different church leaders, I have noticed how little conversation there has been on the actual practices of the Hermanos. Even when their practices are mentioned, the church leaders move the conversation to a discussion concerning obedience, power, and authority. From that first letter exchange between Padre Martínez of Taos and Bishop Zubiría in 1833 the issue of obedience has been the central issue. This isn't particularly surprising. Although there are similarities between the penitential activities of the Hermandad and those of earlier forms of the Christian monastic tradition, as we just described above, the absence of a priestly authority is noticeable. Even after the archbishops of Santa Fe began issuing rules for the Hermanos to follow and requiring all Moradas to join in the Mesa Directiva, there is still no established collaboration between the local priest or pastor included in the actual penitential practices. At this point, our discussion could go in the direction of analyzing more closely the power dynamics between the Penitente Brotherhood and church leaders. While that area does need further exploration, I think it would be unfaithful to the experience Larry is trying to share with us. The issues surrounding power, authority, and obedience may be the main agenda of church leaders, but they are not Larry's, nor that of the Penitentes.

The conversation that we have heard Larry initiating with church leaders numerous times concerns the challenge of "coming to terms with reality" and "making our own peace with ourselves." Reality for Larry is that we are dust; we are both vulnerable and fragile. To be more specific about that reality: we are all going to die and that generates fear in us. Talking with me, he described his experience in relationship to a conversation he had with Georgia O'Keeffe. He put it this way:

> I learned to love the dark . . . and learned to love that which scares everybody else and as the late [Georgia] O'Keeffe once said to me ah . . . "Learn to see beauty where others can't see it. Forget the obvious beauty, where's the harsh beauty, the brutal beauty, the . . . beauty that demands" . . . and that's what I think Penitentismo is about in a large measure. Finding the solace and the beauty of death, maybe, of dealing with fear.

Through Penitentismo Larry has been able to face his fears, particularly his fear of death. What's powerful about his description of coming to terms with this reality through Penitente practices is the peace that comes afterward. Now, there is beauty in death for Larry. There is solace in dealing with his fear of death. When we look back over Larry's comments in his spiritual life stories, we realize that his process of dealing with his fears is connected to another important dimension of his life.

The reality of his life may be that he was and is dust, but Larry's life is also a matter of striving, of becoming special. In the beginning moments of his sharing his stories with me he said, "The idea or the perception that there is a need to be special or different in some way and you don't know why, you just know you have to or die trying . . . was something made abundantly clear to me." The juxtaposition of this realization that he is dust with the acknowledgment that he needs to be special or different is at the heart of Larry's Penitente spirituality.

In order to help us gain a deeper sense of the dynamic of this juxtaposition in Larry's life, I'd like to offer a point of comparison, from the preface of *Forgetting Ourselves on Purpose: Vocation and the Ethics of Ambition* by Brian Mahan. In this passage, Mahan offers the major premise of his book:

> I am convinced . . . that whether we know it or not—or, better, whether we remember it or not—what we'd most like to do is chuck the whole project of improving ourselves and with it our incessant and obsessive monitoring of our "progress" toward whoever it is we think

we ought to be. That is to say, we long for a kind of self-forgetful yet fully engaged sense of immediacy, for a more graced and gracious way of being in this world, one that cuts deeper than the surface imagery sketched by our infernal preoccupation with some soon-to-be success or failure (financial, social, or spiritual).[12]

In the rest of his book, Mahan explores (and invites the reader to do the same) some of the ways in which we human beings have been re-cruited into programs of self-improvement and have been well-trained in the art of scrutinizing ourselves concerning the extent to which we have achieved success. His premise is, however, that on a deeper level there is the desire to let go of those programs and the preoccupations they prescribe.

Penitente spirituality offers Larry the opportunity to let go of his striving to be something different, something special. It allows him to let go of the preoccupations that surround him in his daily life. At the moment after flagellation, Larry experiences a kind of peace, a mo-ment of grace that is unlike any other. He described it this way:

> That's true humbling of self because regardless of your social status or however intelligent you might think you are, it doesn't matter any-more at that point in history; you are just bone and dirt, you're bones and dust. It is a living death . . . from which there is resurrection. And of course, fifteen minutes later when the light of Christ comes back in and they throw open the doors and all the dead are no longer there, there's nothing but the moon shining down upon you and . . . there's that silence . . . maybe a cricket in the background but . . . silence . . . and nobody says anything. You just kind of shuffle out of the room and realize that regardless of the seasons, regardless of the tides, regardless of your bank job or your school teaching job, at that moment you are starting life all over again. Something that I have never even felt even from the ecstasies of Communion, never as strong as when I am lying on the earth floor . . . I know the priest would not like for me to say that or to hear of it but that's the truth. That's my truth at this moment . . . That's my truth.

Stronger than the ecstasies of Communion is the way in which Larry describes the power in this moment of truth. Here, Larry makes the

---

[12] Brian Mahan, *Forgetting Ourselves on Purpose: Vocation and the Ethics of Ambition* (San Francisco, CA: Jossey-Bass, 2002), xx–xxi.

comparison between his experiences of receiving Communion and his experience of Tinieblas (Tenebrae) to help us understand how significant these Penitente practices are for him. His comparison does something else. It helps us see that programs of self-improvement and self-monitoring are not simply aspects of life outside the church. Being preoccupied with how one ought to be—"I know the priest would not like for me to say that or to hear of it"—is also found inside the church.

Earlier in this chapter we explored the way in which Talal Asad described medieval monastic programs of transforming and reorganizing the Christian self. In comparison, I suggested that Penitentismo, as Larry described it, was more a matter of letting go of what we may consider to be our true selves: wealth, status, occupation. I want to refine my comments one step further, based upon our exploration of Larry's comments. Penitente spirituality is not a matter of *transforming the self*, but of *transforming the way in which we label the self*. The language of transforming or reforming or reorganizing the self suggests making the self into something that it is not already, that is, from sinful to virtuous. For Larry, the challenge is to change the way we view ourselves, that is, from special or fearful to vulnerable. Both processes require a kind of submission and both lead to a kind of humility. They also lead one there by very different paths.

In Asad's account, the self becomes transformed by rigorously monitoring one's sinful condition and submitting to the monastic rule as interpreted by the abbot. Humility is demonstrated through one's willingness to obey. In Larry's account, submission is a matter of facing the truth about our vulnerability and fragility and of confronting the fears of our own death. Humility is demonstrated through one's letting go of the compulsion to become somebody special.

The point of facing our vulnerability and our mortality, according to Larry, is not to transform us into something more. We face it so that we will transform the ways in which we see ourselves. Instead of seeing immortality, we see beauty. We approach with fear and we find solace. Where we encounter death, we find life. By embracing the limitations that come with being vulnerable, Larry encounters the possibility of letting go of the whole project of transforming the self.

After experiencing Holy Week with the Penitentes in Arroyo Seco several times, I started wondering why the Hermanos didn't have any events, other than the election of new officers, beyond their Tinieblas service on the night of Good Friday. To my knowledge, there is no observance of Easter identified with their practices, other than attending Mass in the parish. After talking and reflecting with Larry about his experience, I have learned that at the end of Tinieblas, when the light of Christ is restored, there is a moment of resurrection. At that moment, there is a new beginning. In fact, from Larry's account, life begins anew, not only for Christ, but also for everyone. In the end, however, the celebration of the resurrection doesn't appear to be the central element of the Christian story—or the central miracle—as it is within the wider Christian community. The real miracle, the central element of the story is that there is life *at all*. The fact that we are dust and bones means that we are more like the dead than not. This is the ground of our humility. Even as dust, we are alive. Even alive, we remain dust.

BEYOND RESTORING PRIMARY THEOLOGY

In the introduction I cited Aidan Kavanagh's invitation to theologians (and other academics too) to get off the "tourist bus" and to allow ourselves to be caught up in the activities of the world. In other words, he invites us to stop analyzing Christian life from a distance and to engage it where Christians live it. I am not sure how far Kavanagh intends his metaphor to be taken. Maybe he doesn't offer it as a metaphor at all. Perhaps he means just what he says. That's the way I have interpreted his invitation.

But what are we to pay attention to when we venture out into the roads, the plazas, and the courtyards? According to Kavanagh, we should be paying attention to the *structure* of the activities; how it works, what we create with that structure, and what we discover about reality through it.[13] In particular, Kavanagh is interested in what Christians are doing when they gather together. What are they saying? How are they praying? What are they doing? This is why he calls the members of the Christian community primary theologians. They are the ones who are performing the actions, and they are the ones

---

[13] Within theology and sociology there are ongoing debates about whether Christian rituals should be understood primarily as transformative practices or primarily as metaphors. Although an investigation into Kavanagh's position on this would be worthwhile, it is beyond the scope of this book. For a review of the perspectives on this topic, see Nathan Mitchell, "Revisiting the Roots of Ritual," *Liturgy Digest* 1, no. 1 (Spring 1993): 4–36. For a more recent discussion of this debate, see Asad, *Genealogies of Religion*, 126–47.

who are encountering God and one another in their gathering. The reflections that flow out from those experiences are also theology for Kavanagh. He calls that secondary theology.[14]

As we saw in the introduction, Kavanagh's central interest includes restoring the ritual life of the Christian community to its place of primacy within theology, and with that, restoring Christians to their role as primary theologians. Kavanagh's vision, however, needs to be significantly expanded, if not completely altered. The first expansion includes not limiting our critical reflections to what are considered to be the core rituals, the "official rites," of the Christian community, primarily the sacraments.[15] The point here is not to challenge what should or shouldn't be considered under the heading of ritual. My interest, rather, is to expand the boundaries of what "counts" as primary theology. Why should we not pay attention to the experiences of the people working in the kitchen, praying their rosaries, cleaning the church, fasting from food, or whipping their bodies, if they are telling us that they see these practices as part of their relationship with God? I have yet to hear a convincing argument. Even if we don't perform that particular practice or we are not inclined to see the benefit of the practice, theologians are obligated to pay attention. In this way I propose that ethnographic study will decenter "official" rites and refocus our attention on the whole web of practices within a community: liturgical, devotional, and everyday.

Furthermore, Kavanagh's argument suggests that the structure of the worship life of the community is singular. That is to say, there is one structure by which Christians join together in worship. This is simply not true. In the case of Arroyo Seco, the structure of their communal activities shifts depending on the perspective of the participant. Each one selects which events he or she will attend. Those choices are then integrated into the repertoire of practices of that particular participant. Additionally, these structures shift not only from person to

---

[14] Within the academy we call the people who do this critical reflection "theologians." We don't call them "secondary theologians," but perhaps we should call them "professional theologians."

[15] Of course, the category of *sacrament* is not interpreted universally within Christianity. There are a variety of perspectives concerning which rituals are considered sacraments. And, even if we considered Eucharist/Communion and baptism to be the two rituals most widely praticed, we would still need to admit that some traditions do not practice either of these.

person but also from year to year within the community. The repertoire of activities and events of the parish in Arroyo Seco has changed over the years. Two recent examples would be the addition of the Divine Mercy devotion and the addition of the Penitente El Sermón del Descendimiento, which reenacts the removal of Jesus' body from the cross.

This leads directly to the second way in which I am seeking to expand Kavanagh's vision. Secondary theology, that is the critical reflection on the relationship between God and the Christian community, must include the ways in which the participants interpret and narrate their experiences. Critical reflection on the structures alone is not sufficient. Kavanagh suggests focusing on the structures because they are more enduring. To paraphrase him, the structures far outlast the meanings we attach to them. The meanings, however, are more than attachments.[16] They are central to the way in which people engage the structures. If the meanings of the practices do change for people (and they do), theologians should be aware of and account for these shifts. In part, those meanings shift in relationship to the other activities and experiences that the participants bring to communal activities. For example, in Larry's comments we see that his relationship with Georgia O'Keeffe noticeably shaped the way in which he interpreted his experience of being a Penitente at this point in his life.

When we look at the research presented in this book, we see a clear illustration of my rationale to expand Kavanagh's vision. In the case of the Penitente practices in Arroyo Seco, we see one way in which the official rituals of the church and the activities sponsored by the Penitentes literally intertwine with one another. For the Penitentes and the others who join them in their activities, any analysis that looked only at the "official rituals" would have an inaccurate picture of the life of this parish community. Furthermore, if we were to add the Penitente activities to the list of "official rituals" we would have a more accurate starting place for critically reflecting on the structural elements of their community life, but we would still have an incomplete context for critical reflection. The variety of experiences and meanings that is

---

[16] For further discussion about how liturgical piety has historically affected the "key" in which participants experienced the liturgy and consequently affected liturgical structures, see Alexander Schmemann, *Introduction to Liturgical Theology*, trans. Asheleigh E. Moorehouse (1966; repr., Crestwood, NY: St. Vladimir's Seminary Press, 1996), 97–98, 142–44.

created through their participation in this particular context would be lost.

Some readers may welcome the expansion of liturgical theology to include the many other activities that compose the multiple structures of a particular Christian community, but remain unconvinced about paying attention to the lived experiences of the participants. Such critics could suggest that critical reflection on this level will yield, at best, discrete insights appropriate for a particular individual. This level of reflection would offer no insight beneficial to the wider community. I suspect Kavanagh would be one such critic. Using the research presented here as an example, this kind of criticism could suggest that what we have learned about Larry's experience of being a Penitente helps us understand Larry, but it doesn't help us understand the parish community or the Arroyo Seco Morada very well. Such evaluation could also claim that Larry's experience can't be generalized. That is to say, we can't take Larry's experience as indicative of the way in which everyone experiences the activities of the parish community. Looking at the participants in the Penitente activities alone we see several different kinds of participants: the Verónicas, the Auxiliadoras, the visitors, the pilgrims, and the clergy. Among and within each of these categories there could be multiple interpretations and experiences.

I raise these criticisms because they are real and because they can help us focus more directly on why it is important and necessary for professional theologians to move beyond the boundaries of liturgical theology as presented by Kavanagh. The underlying issue to which these criticisms point is the matter of our motivation(s) for doing ethnographic research. As I clearly stated in the introduction, my motivation for promoting ethnographic research was not a matter of proposing an alternative method of gathering data about the people in our communities or denominations that we can use in creating future programming or worship services. Nor am I suggesting that we can use the experiences of one informant, no matter how articulate he or she may be, as a way to generalize about an entire group of people. My assumption is that there are multiple experiences and interpretations within one group or subgroup of participants. My motivation has been to subvert the assumption that there is only one way for Christians to worship, pray, practice, and believe. The truth is that we all don't agree on a single way to be Christian.

In the case of the Penitentes in Arroyo Seco, my reason for talking and reflecting with Larry was not to arrive at the way in which

Penitente practices are experienced in Seco. The motivation was to understand more clearly how he experienced and interpreted them and to begin the process of finding out the various ways in which those activities are experienced. In Larry's particular case, we have the additional element of his being one of the catechists for the Seco Morada and one of the public interpreters of Penitente practices in the Taos Valley. While this means that he could have some influence in how others experience Penitentismo, it doesn't mean he speaks on behalf of others. I would also remind the reader that this project was not a full ethnographic study. It was the beginning of what could be a more comprehensive study. A full study would probably explore the extent to which Larry does influence the experiences of other participants.

Wanting to learn from others about how they experience their everyday lives, what activities they associate with their relationship with God, and why they interpret those activities in the way that they do could be a powerful motivation for a professional theologian or a pastoral minister to consider engaging ethnographic research. As Christian theologians and pastoral ministers, there is another, more profound aspect of ethnographic research. Let us take our discussion there in these final pages.

ETHNOGRAPHY AS A THEOLOGICAL PRACTICE

In the early stages of research in Arroyo Seco I was reading the ethnographic studies by Lila Abu-Lughod, Robert Orsi, Elaine Lawless, and Karen McCarthy Brown. In their own ways, each author proposes that ethnographers need to ask themselves why they have chosen to study a particular field site. If theologians and pastoral ministers intend to do ethnographic research, they must also engage this question, even if they have no intention of ever publishing their research or presenting it to a public audience. Related to this question are many practical, methodological, ethical, and spiritual/theological considerations. While all these considerations are worth exploring, I'll limit myself to exploring the spiritual/theological dimensions of ethnographic research that I see.

At the advice of these well-known ethnographers, I asked myself numerous times throughout my research why I had chosen Arroyo Seco and Larry as the context for doing ethnographic research. My responses changed over time. They were often colored by what was happening at that particular moment in the research process. I'd like

109

to say that I began researching the Penitentes in Arroyo Seco because I was sympathetic to the pain they have experienced at the hands of church leaders. That wasn't the case. I was motivated initially to do my research there because I found their way of practicing Catholicism very different from my own. Over time, however, my motivation was transformed through the process of doing ethnographic research in that community, and particularly through interviewing and talking with Larry. Ethnographic research became a theological and spiritual act for me.

As I spent more time in the village of Seco and with the Penitentes, I was captivated by their story of surviving the attempts of church leaders to suppress them and their practices. For nearly a century, this community of penitents continued their practices without church approval. When I had experienced for myself what it was like to be rejected by the church, as I described in chapter 3, I encountered, in an immediate way, the suffering that is incurred when we refuse to take seriously the experiences of others. When Larry created the opportunity for me to speak openly about my life, we entered into a deeper conversation. We were *listening to each other*. He was no longer my "informant." We became conversation partners.

In this particular research context, I was a Roman Catholic priest and an academic theologian doing ethnographic research with the Penitentes of Arroyo Seco, a group within my own denomination who has had a very tumultuous history with our church leaders because of the spiritual practices they perform. My role as an ethnographer entailed learning about their practices and their relationship with those practices. In the words of Robert Orsi, "The point is . . . to bring the other into fuller focus within the circumstances of his or her history, relationships, and experiences."[17] Part of this task was a matter of reflecting deeply over time with people about their experiences of their spiritual practices. In my conversations and interviews with Larry, he was reflecting with me about how he had come to know himself and God through Penitentismo. Our time of reflecting together was certainly an act of secondary theology. We were discerning together about how his Penitente practices had helped him face the reality of his life and the presence of Christ in the midst of that reality.

[17] Robert A. Orsi, *Between Heaven and Earth: The Religious Worlds People Make and the Scholars Who Study Them* (Princeton, NJ: Princeton University Press, 2005), 8.

As I pointed out above and detailed in chapter 3, my conversations with Larry were not simply a matter of my listening to Larry talk about his life. We talked about my life too and the ways in which I was coming to terms with my own reality and the presence of God in the midst of my life. In part, what I am describing is similar to what Elaine Lawless calls "reciprocal ethnography." In describing the method she says the following:

> [Reciprocal ethnography] takes "reflexive anthropology" one step further by foregrounding dialogue as a process in understanding and knowledge retrieval. The approach is feminist because it insists on a denial of hierarchical constructs that place the scholar at some apex of knowledge and understanding and her "subjects" in some inferior, less knowledgeable position. This approach seeks to privilege no voice over another and relies on dialogue as the key to understanding and illumination.[18]

Larry and I were offering each other a space and context in which we could reflect on and discern our own lives and the presence of God.

From a theological perspective, I think Lawless's definition allows us to go one step further. Ethnographic research can also be an act of primary theology. When we theologians and pastoral ministers enter into a conversation with other members of our denominations and share the details of our daily lives and the ways in which we have experienced God, something more than "knowledge retrieval" or even the emergence of knowledge is happening. This is most striking when the people we are inviting into the conversation have been asked by the denomination to keep silent about the very ways in which they have experienced the grace of God. We are creating a space together, charged with, in the words of Robert Orsi, "an attitude of disciplined openness and attentiveness." Here, the theologian or pastoral minister sets aside the hierarchical constructs that so often govern the relationships between pastor and parishioner, clergy and layperson, theologian and average Christian. The point of the conversation is not to evaluate the extent to which the practitioners are doing what they should be doing or the extent to which they have become the people

---

[18] Elaine Lawless, *Holy Women, Wholly Women: Sharing Ministries Through Life Stories and Reciprocal Ethnography* (Philadelphia: University of Pennsylvania Press, 1993), 4–5.

they are supposed to become. The point is to create a context where the reality of their lives and ours can emerge, without the threat of condemnation and obliteration. When this happens, lives and relationships are transformed.

The course of my research in Arroyo Seco was distinctly influenced by the particularities of my situation and that of the Penitentes. The secrecy imposed on the Hermandad by church leaders, my departure from Roman Catholic ministry, and Larry's established pattern of self-reflection were all factors that influenced the way in which I was able to do ethnographic research in that context. These circumstances allowed Larry and me to enter into a reciprocal relationship. Theologians working in other contexts and with other factors may shape their research differently. They may, or may not, be able to enter into a similar pattern of reciprocal conversations, but they may be more able to partake freely in the activities of their research participants. In my case, I was not able to participate completely in the activities of the Penitentes. Consequently, the verbal dimensions of my research, for example, interviews and spiritual life stories, became essential to the project.

CONCLUDING REMARKS

I opened the introduction with an accounting of my experience of the programmatic theological education that I received at the Katholieke Universiteit Leuven while preparing for ordination in the Roman Catholic Church. In that accounting I outlined the pattern of that education and how it shaped me and some of the ways in which I understood my roles as priest and pastoral minister and as theologian. Like my classmates from around the world, I was taught that we entered the theology program without sufficient knowledge to engage our professors about the lectures delivered to us. Questions, comments, and discussion were not appropriate. After several years of coursework and paper writing we were finally granted the opportunity to enter into conversation with our professors. Even then, those conversations were extremely limited. The intention of the program was to send us out as experts in the field of theology and as capable teachers. Our professors hoped that we would pass on the knowledge that we received to the members of our parishes and the students in our classrooms. The transfer of knowledge by a competent and authorized theologian was held in equal if not greater esteem, as the transfer of grace by a competent and authorized pastoral minister.

I began this work with that narrative for two reasons. First of all, I wanted to offer the reader a wider view of the trajectory of my perspective on theology and theological education. By proposing that theologians and pastoral ministers should be utilizing the tools of ethnographic research (e.g., interviewing, focus groups, spiritual life stories, participant observation), I am not proposing that we dispense with courses in church history, liturgy, ethics, Scripture, or systematic theology. I am proposing that traditional programmatic theological education ignores a critical element of theology at the risk of diminishing the point of its claim.

Second, I wanted the reader to have a point of comparison when I describe how ethnographic research can be both an act of secondary theology and of primary theology. Kavanagh's vision of restoring the liturgical life of the Christian community to its place of primacy within the discipline of theology has not come to pass. In part, that's the case because Kavanagh, with the help of other theologians and anthropologists, drew a small circle around what should be included as primary theology. The other difficulty has been that theologians and church leaders have been slow to set aside the hierarchical constructs that privilege their interpretations and life experiences and even slower to enter into reciprocal dialogue with practicing Christians who are different from themselves.

My research with the Penitentes in Arroyo Seco and, in particular, with Larry Torres, was intended to be a "live" illustration of my argument. In the end, I think it has been that and more. My decision to become more transparent with Larry about my life and struggles of faith led me into a more reciprocal conversation with Larry. While that decision reflected my willingness to take a risk, it is not particularly praiseworthy. That was the least I could offer him. How could I hope that he would be open with me if I was not willing to be open with him? Larry's willingness to share with me how his Penitente practices have helped him come to terms with his fragility and his fears did more than help me to see him and his practices more clearly. He challenged me to face my own fears, vulnerabilities, and preoccupations. He did that by inviting me to come out from behind my roles as "Father" and "theologian" and see that I too am dust.

When researchers transform ethnographic study from being a method of data gathering into being an opportunity to enter into reciprocal relationships with research participants, the researchers and the research participants create the possibility of *knowing* each other and *being known* by each other. For this transformation to happen, the researcher must set aside whatever constructs or behavioral patterns that would privilege his or her voice or participation in the field. The point is not for the researcher's voice to become silent, but to enter into dialogue with the participants' voices. Consequently, the "disciplined openness" that is required of the researcher becomes a crucial element in establishing a context in which each voice can be heard.

Integrating ethnographic research into liturgical theology and theological studies places very particular demands on the theologian and the pastoral minister. If we truly want to know how our Christian companions live and interpret their everyday lives, we must be willing to set aside our assumptions that we are the only experts and that we already know how life is for them. Instead, we must be willing to join them—in conversation, in reflection, and in the activities of their lives. In the process, we will learn more about who we are and who we are together.

The Feast Day of
Nuestra Señora de los Dolores[1]

INTRODUCTORY REMARKS

The following account of the feast day of Nuestra Señora de los Dolores is based on my observations from participating in the celebrations in September 2002. This feast day is another aspect of the yearly cycle of events in the life of the Holy Trinity Parish. I have included this description for several reasons. First of all, it helps us to see how the encounter between Mary and Jesus, which we described in chapter 2, is revisited again in September, when the parish focuses on the other sorrowful events in the life of Mary. In addition, the active participation of the Penitentes in the feast day celebrations in Arroyo Hondo offers us another view of the way in which they interact with the larger parish community. The feast day this particular year included Larry addressing the members of the parish and the priest about how they were interacting. We see him, once again, in his role as community leader and commentator. At the end of this appendix, I outline aspects of this celebration that warrant further attention in future studies.

HISTORICAL BACKGROUND

Nuestra Señora de los Dolores is a popular patron saint in northern New Mexico. The feast day originated in Germany in 1413 (the Synod of Cologne). At that time the feast, which was celebrated during the third week of Easter, focused specifically on the suffering and sorrow of Mary during Jesus' crucifixion and death. Eventually the feast day was extended throughout the Roman Catholic Church and was expanded to include seven moments of sorrow within the life of Mary: the prophecy made by Simeon that Mary's heart would be pierced, the flight of the Holy Family into Egypt, the losing of the child Jesus while in Jerusalem, the encounter with Jesus on the way to crucifixion,

---

[1] Our Lady of Sorrows.

standing at the foot of the cross while Jesus dies, watching Jesus' body being taken from the cross, and the burial of Jesus. Presently, in the Roman calendar, the feast day of Our Lady of Sorrows is September 15. In particular instances, the commemoration of the feast day can be shifted to another day.

THE FEAST DAY IN ARROYO HONDO

The church in Arroyo Hondo, one of the churches that composes Holy Trinity Parish, is dedicated to Nuestra Señora de los Dolores. The parish, then, celebrates its feast day on her feast day. The feast is marked with a series of events that spans the course of two days. The night before the feast day parishioners gather at the church for a Vespers service, the crowning of the fiesta queen, and a procession with music, prayers, and the lighting of seven luminarias (fires) commemorating the Seven Sorrows. The Penitentes play an active role in festivities. On the feast day itself, the parish celebrates with Mass and a fiesta of music, food, and dancing.

The year I participated in the celebrations the feast of Nuestro Señora de los Dolores landed on a Sunday. I arrived in Seco at 5:45 on Friday afternoon, thinking that I was arriving a day early. While driving from the airport, I called my host to tell him of my safe arrival and he informed me that the priest had changed the schedule of events for the patronal feast and that the Vespers and Penitente procession were going to happen on Friday night instead of Saturday night. My host reported that the new priest was afraid that if they had the vespers on Saturday evening, the people wouldn't come to Mass the following morning. So he decided to do these prayers on Friday evening.

The rain that evening didn't deter the Hermanos from arranging the ocote pine wood in seven stacks around the edges of the church property. The seven woodpiles were for the luminarias, which would become the seven stations used in the procession. The church property consisted of an adobe church with a walled-in courtyard in front of it and a gravel parking lot behind it. The nineteenth-century adobe church, which held about one hundred people, had just recently been restored. The walls were strengthened, the floors refinished, and the altar screen was completely restored. The Stations of the Cross hung on the two sides of the nave.

In the sacristy some of the Hermanos were discussing the arrangements for the procession. In the body of the church people were assembling. The reigning and retiring fiesta queen, a girl of about thirteen years of age, and her court of young girls of similar age, were already seated in the reserved seats on the left side of the church. Two mayordomos[2] moved the statue of Nuestra Señora de los Dolores from her wooden niche on the left side of the sanctuary to a table in front of the altar. In front of her they placed an arrangement of seven red roses and fifteen white carnations the priest had ordered and later interpreted during the service. Below the sanctuary step the Hermanos arranged seven hand-painted images on wood, which depicted each of the Seven Sorrows of Mary.

Just before Vespers was to begin, the Hermanos and the fiesta queen's court gathered at the entrance of the church for the opening procession. The Hermanos led the procession into the church while singing an alabado. The queen's court, in white dresses and shoes, followed behind them. The priest, in an alb, stole, and black cope, and the deacon, in alb and stole, followed at the end of the procession. Following the photocopied sheets, the priest led the community in Vespers. As planned, before the final blessing and dismissal, the priest asked the community to be seated for the crowning of the fiesta queen.

A young mother went to the front of the church and asked the retiring fiesta queen and the new queen to come forward. As they came forward, the woman explained the role of the fiesta queen in representing the community. The woman then invited the girls to address the gathering. Both girls thanked the community for the opportunity to serve and to represent the church and thanked the girls who served as their court. The retiring queen, carefully balancing herself with a crutch she was using, took off her cape and crown and placed them on the new queen. The congregation applauded. At that moment the priest stood up and walked over to the lectern and addressed the community. He suggested to the congregation and the new queen that the job of the fiesta queen was demanding. He pointed out that the retiring queen didn't have a crutch when she was crowned last year. "So be careful," he said, "you could be on two crutches next year!" The people broke into laughter.

---

[2] Mayordomos are the stewards of the local church. They are a common characteristic of the Catholic parishes in New Mexico. In Holy Trinity Parish the pastor invites different individuals or families each year to become mayordomos. Cleaning the church, decorating the church, opening and closing the church, and taking care of the church grounds are among their responsibilities.

117

As the congregation quieted down, Larry Torres got up to the lectern to speak about the history of the Penitentes and their role in New Mexican life. "The roots of the Penitentes go back to Anthony in the desert," Larry began. And he proceeded by saying how penance was also practiced by St. Benedict and St. Francis. "It was the Franciscans who trained the Penitentes to become leaders of the community." This became particularly important when the Franciscans turned their attention to converting the Native Americans in the region and the lack of priests became more severe.

This was similar to the talk that I had heard Larry give many, many times before. But this time he was talking a little faster than usual and his voice had a nervous edge. He went on to retell the story of how the first archbishop of Santa Fe was the Frenchman Jean Baptiste Lamy. "Lamy," Larry said, "lacked respect for Spanish culture and language." When Lamy saw the adobe churches of New Mexico he declared them to be "mud pie" churches and he called for the New Mexican churches to become more like the churches in France. To illustrate how the French influences had reached even this village church, Larry pointed out the French-style Stations of the Cross on the wall and the pointed arch windows that replaced the traditional square, adobe windows.

Lamy, Larry continued, was also the one responsible for excommunicating Padre Martínez of Taos and for getting Pius IX to condemn the Penitente Brotherhood in 1852. At that time the brothers moved their chapter room, which had been connected to the church, adobe by adobe, to a new location across the street. From this location the Penitentes continued their penitential practices. Witnessing to these events, Larry added, was a papal medal of Pius IX that had recently been found during a renovation of the mother church in Seco. The image was found face down in the dirt, underneath one of the columns.

Finishing his historical account, Larry took in a deep breath and said, "Many, many people have called me, complaining about the new priest and the changes. And I can't sleep." Then he addressed the priest and the people saying that the priest needed to "learn to listen" and that the people needed to "learn to hear." He concluded by asking all to pray so that they could begin their fiesta without rancor in their hearts. As he returned to his seat with the Penitentes he led the congregation in several prayers, including an act of contrition.

The Hermanos began an alabado as they organized themselves for the procession. Seven Hermanos picked up the sorrowful stations, and the lead singer led the congregation out to the first luminaria in the front courtyard. Behind the Penitentes came the fiesta queen and her court, the congregation, and the priest and deacon at the very end. By the time the procession had begun, the rain had subsided and it was completely dark. Before the procession arrived at each of the seven luminarias (fires), an Hermano doused the ocote wood with lighter fluid and started the fire. The ocote wood, which is traditionally used for luminarias, smelled almost sweet in the night air.

Each of the seven stations around the church property followed a similar pattern. As we arrived at the fire the Hermanos finished the alabado verse they were singing. The Hermano holding the appropriate sorrowful station would lift it high and the leader would recite a brief account of the particular sorrow that occurred in Mary's life. As the leader went into a brief prayer, he would cue the young girls to throw confetti from their baskets into the flames. Small pieces of newspaper clippings and coupons burned and floated above the crowd.[3] Afterward, the assembled group recited several Hail Marys, an Our Father, and a Glory Be to the Father before processing to the next station, singing the next verse of the alabado. The Hermano song leaders sang the verses of the alabado, and the rest of the Brothers responded with the refrain. Only a few of the older women in the crowd sang along with the Brothers in the refrain. Interspersed with the alabado music were the giggles of the young girls and their mothers shushing them. The rest of us listened as we walked. The daylong rain had left the dirt roads and paths around the church muddy and puddle-ridden. The young girls dressed in white were lifting their dresses to keep them from getting dirty and the older members of the crowd steadied themselves on the arms of loved ones. Trying to avoid falling into a big puddle, one woman grasped my coat to regain her balance. There were a few more women than men in the crowd of about sixty participants that night, but there were people of every age among them. The priest and deacon followed behind the crowd, attentive, but silent.

I noticed that as we processed around the church there was a photographer taking pictures of the procession and of the gatherings at each of the luminarias. I had assumed that the Penitentes had asked her to

---

[3] I learned afterward that years earlier the young girls threw flower petals. When flower petals became too expensive, they began using newspaper clippings.

take the photographs. I found out later that was not the case. Nor had she asked permission to record the event. The Penitentes, however, did not prevent her from taking pictures of the procession. I was surprised by the picture taking because the Hermanos typically disallow any picture taking of their practices.

After the last fire was lit and the seventh sorrow of Mary was re-called, the Hermanos led the group back into the church for the final blessing. Before Father could give the blessing several people came forward to make announcements. The first came from an Hermano from a nearby town who extended the best wishes and blessings of his church to this community on the occasion of its feast day. The second set of comments came from the organizer of the fiesta, who expressed his hopes that the fiesta would be both a spiritual and a social event for the community. He also expressed how happy he was that they had begun the weekend fiesta with a spiritual event. He concluded by inviting people to gather outside under the tent for coffee, donuts, and music. Then, just as the priest was standing to give the blessing, Larry suddenly got up and announced that I was there visiting, doing research on religious practices of northern New Mexico and their rela-tionship to the clergy. He told the community that I would be around the next few days and may approach them with questions. He encour-aged them to talk with me and asserted that I was "trustworthy." At this point, the priest did get up and came forward, saying that he had planned to make some comments, but that enough had already been said. Instead, he gave the blessing and the dismissal.

After the services the priest and deacon returned to the sacristy to disrobe while the members of the congregation greeted one another and talked in the body of the church. Several older women called Larry over to them and thanked him for his comments. A young mother started gathering the new fiesta queen and her court for pic-tures in front of the altar. The deacon, whom I had met many times before, returned to the pews and invited me into the sacristy to meet the new priest. After introductions, the pastor said that I was welcome to use the guest room in the rectory if I ever needed it.

CONCLUDING REMARKS

A larger ethnographic study would need to explore this event in greater detail. Here, however, I will highlight two particulars. The first is the way in which the various elements of the life of the parish are woven together in this feast day. The parish brings together in one event, a Vespers service, a presentation on local church history, the crowning of the fiesta queen, and the Penitente procession. We see too in the service how leadership was shared that night by the pastor, the woman conducting the crowning, Larry, and the Penitentes. The second detail I want to highlight is from the Penitente procession. At each of the seven stations, the young girls threw pieces of newspaper clippings into the luminarias. No one offered interpretive comments on this aspect of the service, either during the service or afterward. I, however, kept thinking about what was written on those paper clippings: news stories of the day, obituaries, birth announcements, wedding pictures, money-saving coupons, and the countless ads bearing the hopes and dreams of so many people. All were tossed into the fires, quickly burned above our heads, and disappeared into the night sky. I was reminded, once again, during my time in Arroyo Seco and the surrounding villages about how temporary and fragile life is. Everything passes away.

Appendix 2

The First Night of Las Posadas[1]

INTRODUCTORY REMARKS

Each year on December 15, the people of Holy Trinity Parish begin their novena to the Santo Niño in preparation for Christmas. For nine nights the community is invited to a different house to commemorate the story of Mary and Joseph searching for a place to stay the night in Bethlehem. Hermano Torres not only leads the devotion, but also translated the text from Spanish to English, organized the flow of the service, and published the booklets that the participants use for the ritual.[2] The service is composed of several parts: the procession, las posadas at the door, prayers and litanies to the Santo Niño, and the ceremony of co-parentship. Interspersed among these elements, Hermano Torres adds commentary and tells stories through which he offers his interpretation of the practice and makes connections to other elements of the community. The service closes with the singing of the song, "Cuando del Santo Niño." The following account is my interpretation of the first night of Las Posadas, which took place in San Cristóbal, December 15, 2002.

LAS POSADAS IN SAN CRISTÓBAL

When Hermano Torres, his parents, and I arrived at the church of San Cristóbal, one of the other villages that belongs to Holy Trinity Parish, the sun had already set. Larry removed the handmade costumes for Mary and Joseph, the baby-doll Jesus, and a stack of Las

---

[1] La posada in Spanish means shelter, lodging, or house. A synonym for la posada is la morada.

[2] Both the Spanish text and the English text are taken directly from the booklet prepared by Larry. The English text is not an exact translation of the Spanish. It is an interpretation of the text created to fit the tune used with the Spanish text. On this night Larry used the Spanish text. He decides each night which text will be used.

Posadas booklets from the plastic tub in the back of his car. Inside the church several families were waiting for Hermano Torres to arrive. Once the young girl and boy were dressed in their tunics and cloaks to look like Mary and Joseph, the group set out to find the home of the host family. As we drew near to the house farolitos lined the dirt road and led us to the parking places in a nearby field.[3] A small luminaria of ocote pine wood was burning outside the house and a few children were dancing around it.

There were approximately forty-five people gathered for the first night of Las Posadas that year. Hermano Torres asked half of us to be the outside chorus accompanying Mary and Joseph. The other half were the inside chorus joining the owners of the home. Just before the procession began, Hermano Torres addressed the "outside pilgrims." He thanked us for coming, and said to those of us standing in the cold "We're going to do the, the *real* sacrifice, the prayer outside. We're going to walk to the fire, very slowly, singing 'La Procesión de Las Posadas'" (emphasis his). Accompanied by a single guitar, the group began singing in Spanish,

> Hermosa Señora,
> Bella peregrina,
> Danos tus auxilios,
> Oh Madre Divina.
>
> Ya van caminando
> Los esposos santos
> Vamos almas todas,
> Siguiendo sus pasos.[4]

We continued to sing as we slowly made our way up the dirt driveway and over to the ocote fire. As we approached the door of the home, we sang,

> Danos Oh Señora,
> Ya tu bendición,

[3] "Farolito" means little lantern. They are composed of a candle inside a paper bag. The candle is secured by a small amount of sand. They are most often used to line a pathway, but they can also be carried.

[4] "Lovely Lady, beautiful pilgrim, grant us your protection, oh Mother Divine. Like the married saints, traveling already, let us go together, following their ways."

Pues te la pedimos,
Muy de corazón.

Sea la del Padre,
También la del Hijo,
Y en perfecta unión,
El Espíritu Santo.[5]

As instructed by Hermano Torres, the young man dressed as Joseph knocked loudly on the front door. Having received no answer, the outside pilgrims began to sing,

De larga jornada,
Rendidos llegamos,
Y así imploramos,
Para descansar.[6]

The people inside the home responded, singing,

¿Quién a nuestras puertas,
En noche inclemente
Se acerca imprudente,
Para molestar?[7]

This sung dialogue continued for almost ten minutes. Finally, the outside pilgrims said that it was Joseph and Mary looking for a place to stay. Those inside sang,

Entrad, bella Niña,
Tú y tu esposo,
Ésta es vuestra casa,
Que humilde ofrezco.[8]

---

[5] "Grant us, oh Lady, your blessing. With our hearts we ask you. May it be of the Father, Son, and in the perfect union with the Holy Spirit."

[6] "From a long journey, we arrive exhausted, and we humbly implore you for a place to rest."

[7] "Who is it at our door on this inclement night, who approaches imprudently to disturb us?"

[8] "Enter beautiful young maiden, you and your spouse. This is your home, which is humbly offered."

The pilgrims outside sang back,

> No tengáis en poco,
> Esta caridad,
> El cielo benigno,
> Os compensará.[9]

As those inside opened wide the door to the house, they sang,

> Ábranse las puertas,
> Rómpanse los velos,
> Que viene a posar,
> La Reina del Cielo.[10]

Mary, Joseph, and the pilgrims were welcomed inside the house where we could see and smell the buffet of posole, elk stew, fresh bread, and pastries waiting for us. As we entered into the warm and welcoming gathering, we all sang,

> Entren santos
> Peregrinos, peregrinos,
> Reciban esta mansión.
> Que aunque pobre
> La morada, la morada,
> Os la doy de corazón.
>
> Cantemos con
> Alegría, alegría,
> Todos al considerar,
> Que Jesús, José
> Y María, y María,
> Nos vinieron hoy a honrar.[11]

The next part of the devotion was composed of prayers and story-telling. Once everyone had gone inside and gathered in the dining

---

[9] "You have done us no small charity. Gracious heaven will bless you."

[10] "Open the doors, tear up the curtains. The Queen of Heaven comes to dwell."

[11] "Enter holy pilgrims, pilgrims. Receive this mansion. Although it may be humble, this dwelling, this dwelling, we give it to you from the heart. Let us sing with joy, with joy. Together let us reflect upon that Jesus, Joseph, and Mary came to honor us today."

room and kitchen area, Hermano Torres stood at the head of the dining room table and began explaining that Las Posadas came from the eleventh scene of a morality play called *The Summoning of St. Joseph*, which tells the story of how Joseph, out of the one hundred suitors of Mary, became her husband. The story also includes how Joseph and Mary, pregnant with Jesus, traveled to Bethlehem to be counted in the census, but could not find anywhere to stay. Hermano Torres went on to say that the devotion of Las Posadas lasts for nine nights, representing the nine months that Mary carried Jesus in her womb. For the first eight nights the couple is turned away from every door. On the last night, the ninth, they are received. This devotion, then, he explained, is devoted to the Holy Child who was to be born.

Following this brief explanation of the origins of the text of Las Posadas, Larry led the gathering in the recitation of a series of prayers in Spanish: the Prayer to the Holy Child, the Act of Contrition, nine Hail Marys, and a litany to the Holy Child. All of the prayers were printed in their booklet, along with an English translation. Before the Act of Contrition Hermano Torres told the story of St. Christopher and his connection with the Christ Child, because they were beginning Las Posadas that year in San Cristóbal.

After the Act of Contrition, Larry noted that the valleys of northern New Mexico are some of the last places where the folk plays brought by the Franciscans are stilled performed. In particular he noted that just as Mary and Joseph paused three times in the procession to the house that night, so would the procession of the statue of Jesus pause three times for the three falls of Jesus during the Encuentro. Furthermore, just as the pilgrims were refused entrance at the door that night, the Hermanos Penitentes will knock at the door of the church and be refused entrance until Jesus has risen.[12] He added that the belief that supports this parallel symbolism is that no one will enter the gates of heaven until the coming of the light of Christ. He then asked the two women who shared the home to come forward and lead the community in the recitation of the nine Hail Marys, which they did.

As we prayed the Hail Marys, a young boy tried repeatedly to blow out the purple Advent candles that were secured in a Star of David

[12] Although he didn't note it for this gathering, there is another parallel in the celebration of Tinieblas on Good Friday in the Morada. As the people offer prayers inside the Morada chapel with the doors closed, the dead bang at the chapel doors and rattle their chains in hope of being raised from the dead.

candleholder. The child was successful. Following the Hail Marys, Hermano Torres used the presence of the Star of David candleholder to remind those gathered that Jesus was himself Jewish and that he came for both the Jewish people and the Gentiles, as the traditional feast of Christmas of New Mexico (the feast of the Magi) celebrates.

Hermano Torres continued with the lengthy litany to the Santo Niño. Halfway through the litany, he made these comments:

> The stories of the miraculous Santo Niño de Atocha are found in Spanish folklore. It is said that at one time the Christians and the Moors were fighting in Spain—you remember that the Moors had invaded Spain in 711 and had occupied it until 1492. One time when they were fighting in the village of Atocha, which is now outside the great gated city of Madrid, there were men, several wounded on both sides. And there was a little child in the cloak of a little pilgrim who would walk, first curing the Christians and then walk across the battle lines to cure the Moors. Suddenly they realized that the infant Jesus and God does not play favorites. He has come for everybody. So they put down their weapons and they began to pray to the holy child of Atocha. It's also important to remember that in years past there used to be three devils that used to accompany the Posadistas and they would run around and bar all the doors, so that they . . . no one would open the doors. The devils are called Lucifer and Satan and Wiley—Satanás, Luceben, and Astucias. They no longer accompany Las Posadas . . . oh . . . or the Posadistas over here . . . but they do remind us that sometimes even in the holiest of places there is the evil one who's trying to a . . . to a . . . to sow rancor in the form of envy or jealousy or burracheras or what have you—things that keep us from finding ourselves in the Christmas . . . in the . . . a . . . Lenten . . . in the Advent season. And so we pray.[13]

As we completed each section of the litany, Larry added a story or comment before we proceeded to the next section. At one point he added that we were asking to be delivered from "our animal selves" in our prayers. At another, he told the story of how the statue of the Santo Niño came to be found in nearby Chimayó and how many people have been healed by its miraculous powers. We too, Larry suggested, were praying for the assistance of the Santo Niño.

[13] Las Posadas, San Cristóbal, New Mexico, recorded on tape by the author, December 15, 2002.

After completing the litany, Larry noted that many people think that the Posadas is just a matter of partying for the nine nights before Christmas. And while it was indeed a celebration, he advised that the focus of Las Posadas was praying to prepare our hearts for Christmas. Consequently, we were to pray certain prayers and to perform particular actions for the following eight days. According to our booklets, our assignment for the first night of Posadas was to pray "five Our Fathers and five Hail Marys for the intentions of the Holy Father." Additionally, we were to refrain from eating fruits and sweets the following day. The booklet also noted that in doing these things we were preparing a basket of gifts for the infant Jesus. This particular assignment would make "His little shirt."

The next part of Las Posadas was the ceremony of compadrísimo, translated in the booklet as co-parentship. Since Mary and Joseph had brought the baby Jesus into this home, the owners of the home were to become co-padres of the infant. Larry noted that compadrísimo was an important way of establishing good neighborly relationships. Through this practice, no matter to whom the children belong, neighbors become co-parents. So, Larry asked the two women who owned the house to join pinkies with the children playing the roles of Mary and Joseph. Once linked together, Larry led them in a compadrísimo vow, asking them to repeat each line after him. They did the vow first in Spanish and then again in English.

Carretita, Carretón	It was meant right from the start.
Con agujero y sin tapón,	With no stopper, flowing out,
El que se vale a la comadre	We are now kin, this we shout:
O al compadre,	One sole team with one sole cart.
Y luego se desvale,	If from this vow we depart,
Se les parte el corazón.	It would shatter their poor hearts.[14]

Bringing the Posadas prayers to a close, Larry announced the location for Posadas the following night and then led us in the singing

[14] The English interpretation of the vow is the one provided by Larry in the Posadas booklet.

of "Vamos todos a Belén" and "Cuando del Santo Niño."[15] Once the prayers were concluded, the owners of the house invited us to stay and enjoy the food, which was prepared by both them and their guests. Everyone remained for at least an hour eating, drinking, and socializing.

As Larry, his parents, and I returned home that night, they remarked positively on the unusual number of people in attendance for the first night of Posadas. They also noted that the group that night was representative of the village population of San Cristóbal—both Jewish and Christian. Larry said that he had noticed this too. Consequently, he decided to provide more background to the prayers and chose to highlight the Jewish elements of the story. He said he wanted everyone to feel welcome. Each night the celebration of Las Posadas has a different character, Larry explained to me. Each one prompts different kinds of commentary and allows for different stories to be told.

EMERGING PATTERNS AND
POINTS FOR FUTURE RESEARCH

Like the feast day of Our Lady of Sorrows, the celebration of Las Posadas provides us with another dimension of the calendar of events in the life of the parish of Arroyo Seco. As more events, details, and people are added to our view of Holy Trinity Parish we see patterns begin to emerge that would be important for future research in this area. Among those patterns are Larry's role as leader and interpreter of events, the ways in which the services are often crafted to include people from beyond the boundaries of church membership, and the multilayered ways in which the metaphors of home (la morada and la posada) and making a home reappear.

---

[15] "Let Us Go to Bethlehem" and "As the Holy Infant."

Larry Torres' Life Stories[1]

Although I had always known a lot about me and a lot about other people . . . my perceptions have always been pretty good. This man [referring to a lecture on the enneagram] puts very nicely together. And a, the idea or the perception that there is a need to be special or different in some way and you don't know why, you just know you have to or die trying . . . was something made abundantly clear to me. The idea of not being recognized as something different . . . on my terms . . . [DM: uh um] on my terms is abhorrent to me . . . I don't know if you have ever read the letters, the Persian Letters. [. . .]

So I recognize a lot of this in actors. I am trained as a performance artist. I do visual art. I am terrible at media, but I am very good at performance, because I can create an illusion or a persona, almost at will, but not without a great research. I really hate it when somebody says things like a . . . like that guy's a genius. I really hate the term "genius" with every fiber of my being, because calling somebody "genius" cheats them of all the hard work they have put into it—their being what it is they're projecting. I can make something look very easy on stage or on the radio, but suddenly I am off the air and I am in public and people say, "Say something smart." What the hell do you want me to do, think I am expected to be smart on command, to be historically accurate on command, to be culturally savvy on command? And that's another illusion, not just mine, but a lot of

---

[1] This is a transcription of selected portions from the spiritual life stories that Larry recorded with me. Additional comment has been supplied only when necessary. Regarding the editing of the stories, I have used brackets to provide additional information or to indicate unclear words in the recording. I have used ellipses to indicate a slight pause or shift in his comments and ellipses with brackets to indicate where a portion of the text was cut. Larry T. Torres, interview by author, tape recording, Arroyo Seco, NM, December 14–16, 2002.

people will do that. In fact we have talked about the idea that most overnight successes take about fifteen years . . . to get there . . . and you know there is a whole bunch of truth if not total truth in that I know of really know of no one who made it just because overnight. It's the outcome of a struggle. I identify with a lot with the artists of history and a, some of the great writers. Ah, I was thinking of Paul Gauguin right now, when I said it is the outcome of a struggle. When he first came back [. . .] from finding himself from the wild areas like Tahiti, or, or maybe even Taos, New Mexico, you see where people have not been touched in certain ways by civilization. In many ways we are still wild and in many ways we are still medieval in our hearts. And they say, they look at the art and they say, "Oh, that's an interesting notion." Well screw them, it's much more than a notion, it's the outcome of a struggle. And you don't realize that in great art. It's always the outcome of a struggle. Sometimes the outcome of violence. Sometimes it's the outcome of a quest for search, a search for self, or a search for a personality, a persona of some sort. Now that I have the leisure to pursue these things, I ah, I do enjoy thinking about them and thinking, "Wow, who would have thought about that, even ten years ago or even twenty years ago. That I'd be living here in the middle of a cow pasture, the cow pasture where I grew up and it's changed, because out of sheer force of will." I'll look around my house and think; all of this came out of my mind somehow. This house cannot stand the way it stands if I had not designed it in my mind, because it was not one, not on paper. And it makes me marvel at the inventiveness of . . . humanity . . . not just my own inventiveness, but the inventiveness of humanity. I think, I think the big, the biggest tragedy . . . of most men . . . and I use that in the generic sense . . . is the fact that they are not aware of their immediate place in history. I think we all have a place in history and roles to play, but I think when we talk about the great, what do you call that, the . . . the quiet desperation that men are supposed to be leading . . . the desperation doesn't stem from nonaccomplishment; I think it stems more from the idea that they don't recognize their own importance in history and I am not saying that they have to go out and do great battle or design great buildings or build a fantastic statue or build great art, just so you be consciously aware of your place in history. Most people are not. They get up. They go to work. They eat. They sleep. And then they die [pause]. And I think there is something that transcends all this physicality. [. . .]

I identify a lot with Don Quixote de la Mancha, of course, naturally, ah . . . he's the madman amid noblemen or the man amid impoverished noblemen who finds out that he lives in a world of cruelty, a world of deceit, a world of hypocrisy and he doesn't like that. He longs for a time when people were gentle with each other, even if that time never existed, except maybe in his own mind. But maybe that's where it already i . . . the only place it has to exist in his, is in our mind. You know we think of our lives as *cogito ergo est*, "I think therefore you are," instead of, instead of "I think therefore I am," *cogito ergo sum*. [Larry took a phone call.] . . . is the only reality really I think this seventeenth century . . . mathematician said something that is very important even though we just kind of take it for granted. The perception of self . . . is probably the most important factor in coming up with . . . my own, at least my own personal happiness. And I have come to realize that even though other people see the world completely different from what I might see it, I will never compromise them by trying to change them to my way looking at things, to my way of being, to my way of expressing. I usually wait for people to tell me who they are, what they are, if they want to. And if they don't that's fine too, but it's not up to me to say you are this, or to tell somebody he is that or she is that. I think that is a . . . wrong. [Fourteensecond pause; all one hears is the creaking of the wooden chairs.]

I'm a . . . in the middle of a struggle with one of our local priests . . . and a . . . what's interesting about this case is that . . . I see in the man . . . the antithesis of everything else that I thought I was. I don't hate him. I kind of admire him actually, because he's intellectual. But what is interesting is that I've come to realize that just, the sheer intelligence means nothing by itself if it is intolerant . . . I think . . . it is important to be able to reach as many people as possible, really I think that is the reason we are on this earth . . . is to reach. I don't think in the end if there is something called a judgment that we are going to be judged how many times we went to Mass or how many times we didn't. I think it is important . . . to . . . reach, or maybe to love . . . and I'm not again speaking of just a sexual relationship; I am speaking of the idea to open up yourself to as many different ideas, to allow yourself to be vulnerable on occasion and to give others or to afford others the opportunity to be vulnerable in your presence without any kind of judgment . . . and my heart bleeds when I see people who remind me of me at a certain stage in my life where I just couldn't be open to anybody . . . and so how do you reach out to somebody, sometimes you do it by condemning maybe, maybe by telling them that what they are doing is wrong or stupid, a tradition, a cultural is for the weak-minded. All these things and I think what is important to realize is that [. . .] we are all still very much in the developmental stages. Even at the age of ninety-nine, ninety-six, or in my case forty-eight, I'm still just now developing. We say sometimes that we spend a whole lifetime recovering from our childhoods. And some of us never do and maybe we're not meant to. The Don Quixote syndrome again; it doesn't matter whether you reach that unreachable star . . . it is did you follow the quest? And a pretty much just empty words . . . it's something you have to feel in your heart pretty much. But it is . . . and aaaa I was working on an article now that I have yet to finish, in fact I have to finish it by Monday about Pope Pius IX, in which I am coming to the realization that some of the men who have been most intolerant in history or what I have thought close-minded, maybe is wasn't so much intolerance as naïveté or inexperience. So maybe it's in the sharing that you experience, cause you're not really teaching when you're sharing, at least not teaching in the conventional sense of class-room teaching, lecturing, or publishing . . . It's modeling behavior . . . and producing it consciously for somebody else . . . even if you are weak at it. It's the germ of an idea that we have to pass on to some-body else . . . that says a . . . this is what I am trying for, I doubt that I'll succeed but maybe you will. [. . .]

I remember a priest asked me once if I believed in God . . . and he was kind of shocked when I said I believe that there is a God . . . for those who need a God. Something that takes you a little while to realize . . . So the question is "Do you need a God?" . . . Now that is harder to answer than "Is there a God? Do you believe in God?" [DM: Was he asking you?] Uh-huh. [DM: Do you need a God?] No. He didn't ask me. He didn't think that far. He just sat there stunned beyond belief. [I laughed.] I asked myself do I need a God . . . And the answer was . . . I probably do, even if it is only the God within me. I think it is important to recognize the divine in oneself . . . Mod-estly and full of pride at the same time . . . Because I really think that creation, creativity is a gift and . . . I'd like to think when I am doing is that I am reliving the tale of the ten talents—in particular taking tal-ent very literally, but I think that for some reason we do have certain gifts, different gifts, just like every flower out in there in meadow has different petals and different sizes, different sets of roots. And all of them are their different root to the beauty to the harmony of the entire thing . . . if we do their job correctly. And if we are too afraid to move or to express . . . we might as well never have lived. I think the question I am going to ask myself toward the end of my life is more a question of . . . "Did I do what I needed, not only for myself, but for everybody else?" Not, "Did I go to church?" Not, "Did I own a car?" "Did I live in a castle?" Was, "Did I bother to . . . reach out to somebody, in some way? Did it make me a better person? Did that help *them* in some way?" These aren't just Christian ideals; these are fundamental universal truths that need to be spoken and expressed to everybody else. And it doesn't matter what the social status is we have. [. . .]

I rarely talk about these things but I feel myself being carried through space and most of the time I am carried over to that mountain that I see in front of me with the seven falls. And it's like I am gliding I'm just gliding and I am thinking as I am flying, "This is so easy. Why the hell do I bother walking when this is so easy?" And then you wake up and there is a terrible sense of disappointment mixed with euphoria, euphoria because you have . . . slipped the bonds I guess. But disappointment because you realize that you are earthbound in some way and that can't change for you. [Nine-second pause] . . . little things, huh . . . of course sometimes leaving the windows open at night is not the best thing. I'm such fan of [laughing] horror films . . . I was having a Dracula fest once and just as the vampire came in this stupid little bat flew into my bedroom and I go "aaaaa" and then I dive under the covers. It's just a harmless little bat, but the timing was uncanny. And so I finally got the nerve to poke out my head, my head from under the covers. [. . .]

Lot of people think that in order to be happy you have to have this constant contact, but maybe it's because they are projecting their unhappiness onto you. And not comfortable being alone they figure you probably aren't either. Oh . . . gosh . . . how many times have my brothers, my sisters, friends tried to set me up with somebody . . . "just be with somebody." My mother wanted me to advertise and to get some kind of a baby to adopt, so that it could take care of me, and I said, "Mother, there is no guarantee that the babies are going to be around when you're older. There is no guarantee that they're ever going to stay around to take care of you, either. I'm happy. Just . . . be glad for me. Don't pity me. I'm happy with whom I am" . . . but again . . . we all have to make our own . . . peace . . . with our own reality, with our own self. And you can understand it at some intellectual level, but unless you experience yourself, not very likely you'll truly know what it's all about . . . I was given to the service of the Morada when I was nine, my brother Ray was eight; he also joined. Later on he dropped out when he got a girlfriend . . . decided that wasn't for him. Really, we were there to replace my uncle, my godfather, and my grandfather Ga . . . Gabriel? Junior and well my grandfather José Gabriel Marques. I would not recommend that children be allowed into Moradas anymore unless they are past the age of twenty-one . . . but in those days I was somehow recording everything that happened. I'm glad in retrospect that I was so young because it was my nature . . . second nature to me. I grew up really having an experience as a young Penitente, which I think is unparalleled because I have been able to write about it and study it, and analyze it and things I couldn't have done if I were already twenty-one by the time I'd joined. I had lived it. I had just lived it.

I remember the first night in the Morada that we were frightened because we're told the spirits were always out because the Morada is right smack in the middle of the cemetery and we were afraid of the dead. So that there were two Hermanos, two brothers . . . who were designated Hermano Mama, "brother mother," just to take care of the kids. I had never heard that term used in any other Morada . . . but their job, because we were too young to learn, we weren't given to the master of novices, the maestro de novicias, for to teach us our prayers . . . it was the Hermano Mama who'd just take care of us, hold our hand and make sure we weren't afraid. The job of the Hermano Mama was also to take care of the kitchen. No other Penitentes were allowed in the kitchen in those days because we didn't have paper plates or cups. We had twelve cups, twelve forks, twelve spoons, twelve plates, and we fed only twelve people at a time. Since that time now, and the invention of plastic and paper products, we feed thousands, not thousands, excuse me, hundreds of people, scores of people, and they all eat at the same time. It's changed a whole bunch in the . . . forty . . . years that I've been in it. But I remember those days, not as happy days, but as days that were necessary for my own spiritual growth. In my heart, maybe, I have always been some kind of a priest. I never took vows of anything, except to myself. But the Penitente brother-hood had probably much more of an influence on me than [. . .] than I might imagine.

[. . .] I learned to love the dark . . . and learned to love that which scares everybody else and as the late [Georgia] O'Keeffe once said to me ah . . . "Learn to see beauty where others can't see it. Forget the obvious beauty, where's the harsh beauty, the brutal beauty, the . . . beauty that demands" . . . and that's what I think Penitentismo is about in a large measure. Finding the solace and the beauty of death, maybe, of dealing with fear. If you've ever been in a Morada on Good Friday, when the ceremony of Tinieblas is being presented, it's one of the most wonderful things you can imagine. As the lights are being doused one at a time and we pray for the souls of widows and or-phans and people who are jailed or imprisoned, people who have the most terrible will toward us at that moment in time, there's a sense of forgiveness that comes over you, that brings such peace. It's like you're to . . . letting to go not only the hurts brought in from the outside but the hurts . . . brought in from the inside and the hurts you have sent out to everybody else. Maybe not even visible hurts maybe . . . a bad thought you may have had about somebody . . . any you learn to tolerate, or either to accept . . . and suddenly the light of Christ dies out, the *lumen Christi* dies out. The last candle is extinguished and you hear the mourning of the dead as they try to break in. You hear the clanking of the chains, the rattling of the chains. You're all alone in that little room . . . maybe a few people scattered there watching you . . . in the dark and the eyes of the saints are glowing on the altar and for about fifteen minutes you are in limbo, in a very real sense, you're sus-pended somewhere between heaven and hell. It's not a place of suffer-ing. It is not a purgatory. It's not a place of purging. But it is a place of coming to terms with yo . . . reality. It's like being alive in your own tomb, but not trapped because knowing in a few minutes the light will come back.

It's a very pagan ritual. It's almost a fertility ritual. And it is something that I doubt very few people, outside of monks or some few select people in Rome maybe have done, have ever experienced it. It is not a seminary where you just go and read intellectually about theology and try to understand it and preach it. There's a way of feeling it at the very gut level. To be lain on a . . .packed earth floor, on your belly, with no shirt on, feeling the dampness of the earth, smelling it right next to your nostrils, and realizing that that is part of what you are is that very dirt. That you are that dirt. And maybe being whipped a couple of times and trying not to react or not to feel the sting of it . . . is . . . beyond description. It is something that is interior. You can talk about the sensations that you're going through but really, mentally, to feel your own teeth pressed against that soil, as if you were dead, as they pray for your dead brother, your dead family, or whomever and realizing you have joined them somehow physically . . . and mystically . . . is an experience that . . . you couldn't translate to a bunch of students at a university class or a high school class. And to know that it happens every year for forty years, at least at this point . . . wow . . . wow . . . that's true humbling of self because regardless of your social status or however intelligent you might think you are, it doesn't matter anymore at that point in history; you are just bone and dirt, you're bones and dust. It is a living death . . . from which there is resurrection. And of course, fifteen minutes later when the light of Christ comes back in and they throw open the doors and all the dead are no longer there, there's nothing but the moon shining down upon you and . . . there's that silence . . . maybe a cricket in the background but . . . silence . . . and nobody says anything. You just kind of shuffle out of the room and realize that regardless of the seasons, regardless of the tides, regardless of your bank job or your school teaching job, at that moment you are starting life all over again. Something that I have never even felt even from the ecstasies of Communion, never as strong as when I am lying on the earth floor . . . I know the priest would not like for me to say that or to hear of it but that's the truth. That's my truth at this moment . . . That's my truth . . . I enjoy directing all those passion plays because it has taught me that . . . nothing is eternal and that all of these folk plays that we do, regardless of the season of the year because they are cyclical plays . . . I find them much more than sacred drama. I find that they are attempts to come to terms with self as a society . . . or maybe, as just the writer, because we really don't know who put them together in the first place. But, uh . . . but somebody had a longing, a yearning and some way you are connecting to that yearning and possibly not even coming up with the answer to that yearning, but . . . experiencing that yearning to know . . . just the need to know. Not necessarily to be used for any purpose . . . just to know, to be, to heal, to be complete, or to be more complete if not fully complete. [Nine-second pause.]

[. . .] There has been disappointment for me when I look at priesthood. When I grew up, I had the naïve . . . trust that priests were like saints and perfect people, and that's what I wanted to be. And as I grew older and saw that they were irritable, that they were angry, that they were licentious, that they were greedy, avaricious, in short, they were human, and the longing for priesthood kind of diminished in me. And when I grow even older and find out that they're even much more human . . . ah . . . you wonder if such a thing as perfection or divinity is in anyone. Cause that's what I was looking for in myself and hoping that by hanging out with priests I would somehow be guided to it. And then the disappointment that it's not there either . . . kind of unnerving . . . Is there divinity on earth? Unless it's so obvious that I can't see it. And that's the thing I tell everybody. "If something is so obvious, there's no way I'm gonna see it." I can think of a hundred different ways of doing the most obvious job except the easiest and the most simple. And maybe that extends to my spiritual life too, and maybe I never lost it, like Dorothy in *The Wizard of Oz*, who says I wouldn't go looking any farther than my backyard, because if it's not there, maybe I never lost it to begin with. It's a powerful line . . . it's a very powerful line . . . maybe it was never lost to begin with. It's like a baby who is crying for a bottle in night not realizing that it's still there . . . wow. Let's stop there for now. Kinda tired.

[. . .] That Padre Martínez of Taos would be chosen as the obvious first bishop of Santa Fe, but Pope Pius IX had other plans. Under the influence of the apostolic see in Baltimore, Maryland, he chose, at the recommendation of Bis . . . Bishop Purcell of Cincinnati a young Frenchman who had left his home in the Auvergne Valley [. . .] in France, and had come with his . . . his comrade, Joseph Machebeuf to the Ohio Valley at a time when he was only twenty-five, Machebeuf was only twenty-seven. They were very . . . close. Well, what happened was he was given the title of Lord of Agathonica by the grace of God, Lord bishop of Santa Fe. [Larry sneezed.] Well, the first thing he did was when he arrived in Santa Fe was he declared that the Spanish churches here as they were run by the Penitentes, who were the . . . the ordinary lay ministers at the time were not in compliance with what Rome was directing. Pope Pius IX . . . had asked him quietly to disband the Penitente brotherhood and he agreed to do it. And he had the seal of Cardinal Barnable, which . . . was the seal of the . . . Society for the Propagation of the Holy Faith abroad. That carried a lot of weight in those days and he brought it to Pa . . . Padre Martínez of Taos. And Padre Martínez of Taos knew the meaning of that. And he asked him to spare the Penitente Brotherhood because they had kept the holy church alive in New Mexico from 1540 until the present, which was 1850. Three hundred years they had kept it alive at a time when otherwise it might have perished. Cause you have to remember that the Franciscan friars had come to New Mexico to bring the faith to the natives of this area, not to the Spanish. So the Spanish had to fend for themselves and try to figure out their rituals and their meanings. This is why, for example, when you do plays like Los Pastores, the Shepherd's play that I mentioned, you have strange anachronistic elements in it, like, you'll find that the hermit tries to keep the devil away by flashing the cross at him. Well, Jesus hadn't even been born yet, so the salvific power of the cross wasn't even known. Yet it exists in the folk play. The rosary, upon which the cross is attached, well, St. Dominic hadn't invented it yet. At that time . . . at the . . . at the bidding of the Lady of Mount Carmel. So it's, again, anachronistic, the people recognized the symbols but didn't know when they had occurred. So all of these things are important but the new archbishop had little . . . the new bishop rather, had little tolerance for all of these things . . . in that scene you see Padre Martínez and his followers decided, it is said, to test the French church in New Mexico. And so what they did was in the pulpit of northern New Mexico of St. Gertrude of Mora there was a priest, a French priest, named Antoine Avel A-V-E-L, who went to give the morning service once, and he blessed the bread and he pronounced the Greek, the Latin, *hoc est enim corpus meum*—"This is my body"—which has since been corrupted to the words *hoc e-s poc-e-s*, which is what we do when we do . . . magic. Then he took the cup of blood and he a . . . wine and he pronounced it the blood of Jesus *hic est calix meus*—"This is the cup of my . . . blood"—and as he turned to drink the . . . chalice . . . full of wine, transubstantiated into blood he realized that the contents had been replaced by Martínez and his followers with deadliest poison. Now here's the dilemma: to drink the cup means that you'd have to die. Not to drink the cup would mean that the French church in New Mexico was a sham. He chose to drink the cup and he died. Well . . . Padre Martínez thought . . . "Well . . . maybe there is something to be said for this new French church which has come to invade New Mexico." But before he could act, Bishop Lamy sent his sidekick, Joseph Machebeuf, to Taos, with a writ of excommunication. As Padre Martínez approached it, he posted the writ of excommunication and raised the apostolic candle, the . . . the Easter candle over the head of Martínez and that is what that painting represents. As Martínez repre . . . a . . . ah . . . came up, he said in Latin, "*In nomini patris, et filii, et spiritu sancti.* In the name of the Father, the Son and the Holy Spirit, Padre Martínez of Taos you stand excommunicated from Holy Mother the Church and in peril of your immortal soul." And then he took the Easter candle and he plunged it into the font at the front of the church. Immediately the water in the baptismal font began to boi . . . boil and sputter as the soul of Padre Martínez is reported to have fried in hell at that moment. Then Joseph Machebeuf went to the village of Arroyo Hondo and he pronounced the same excommunication over Padre Lucero who was one of the followers of Martínez. Well . . . the people of New Mexico knew a . . . sign . . . when they had seen it and they went away from the church of the Penitentes. Penitentismo was to be driven underground for a long time. But the bishop still wasn't satisfied with the punishment of the people; he needed to chastise them. He said, "I have punished the head of the dragon, now I must punish the body daring to go along with it"—referring to the people. And so he stood on, in 1857 . . . 1856, it is reported, because all I am telling you has not been recorded on paper—at the steps of the adobe cathedral in Santa Fe, and he took a piece of cheese and he held it up and he said, "See this cheese, New Mecas . . . New Mexico, it represents all that we are as a church. And see this knife New Mexico, he said, holding up a big dagger, this represents Padre Martínez of Taos and Padre Lucero of Arroyo Hondo and Padre Salazar of Santa Clara and Padre Gallegos of Albuquerque and Padre Lujan of Santa Fe and Padre Ortiz of Santa Fe. And then he split it in half . . . using the . . . ritual knife. Then he took the right part of the cheese and he held it up, saying, "See how pure it is and how fit for human consumption—this is the French church—take this all of you and eat it, for this is my body." And then he took the other portion of cheese and, "This is the Spanish church, it is vile and corrupt." And however he did it, as he turned the cheese toward them, suddenly the cheese turned to black before their very eyes and crawled with worms. Then he took the two pieces of cheese and put them on the steps of the cathedral, saying choose, New Mexico, the Spanish church or L'eglise francaise. Well . . . the people knew a sign when they had seen it, so they went frock . . . flocking back to the French church and the Spanish church was to be driven underground for a hundred years, not to be resurrected again until the early 1960s by Archbishop Edwin Byrne, who apologized publicly for the wrongs . . . of the church . . . of the Roman Catholic church against the Penitente Brotherhood of New Mexico. So it's important for me to remember all of these details by hanging them out, up there, as art, they remind me of who they are. So if you are still interested in talking about art, we'll do so, but we have only covered one room. [I laughed.] Let's stop there for now.

[. . .] I think the last time we were talking we were talking about the art that's located inside the house. We did the whole living room. [DM: um hum.] Let's move it over to the kitchen for a minute. [. . .]

I used to have a priest friend, turned actor, the late José Rodriguez was with RADA, the Royal Academy of Dramatic Arts in London. He was a protégé of John Gielgud. One day he decided to become a priest in New Mexico and I asked him why. He had founded a Spanish theater company in New Mexico, in Albuquerque, called La Compañía de Teatro. And he had written a play called La Passion de Jesus Chávez in which Jesus is portrayed as a Chicano who has been imprisoned and sits there telling a story that parallels and mimics the life of Christ, in the passion of Christ. One day he was asked to perform this for the peregrinos, the young men and women who walk to Chimayó at the beginning of the summer every year from all four directions of the compass and combine . . . and a . . . come together at the Santuario—seven days later. Well he happened to perform this and in a very real sense he became the Cristo to these young men who were listening to him that night. As he told me that night, he said, . . . "I had performed on many stages but I didn't know that night was to change my life, cause suddenly I finished and there was absolute silence. Then everybody stood up off that gym floor and said (yelling) 'Cristo! Cristo! Cristo!'" And they threw him into the air. He said they kept throwing him into the air. "I was the Cristo in a very real sense to me," he said. "That was my moment of conversion, like St. Paul being hit by a lightning bolt. Suddenly I realized that I could do much better on the altar if I use my theatrical arts for homiletics instead." And he went to Mount Angel Seminary and he . . . was made priest. And it was to change his life. When we were very good friends he was sent to Arroyo Seco, where we kept him in the summer and he . . . helped us found our own theater company, La Santísima Trinidad, of which I became the first director. Well . . . ah . . . he missed his life on stage and he wanted to do more things. I remember the night he was to be ordained, the night before he was to be ordained, we're sitting around talking in Seco and he said, oh yeah, he said, "Tomorrow I become a prince of the church." He said, "My head will be put on a pi . . a silken cushion." And I laughed, and he narrowed his vision, which always meant that he meant business. He said, "What do you want?" And I said, "The church of New Mexico already has too many kings and queens, and princes." He said, "What do you want from me?" I said, "Instead of seeing your face on a silken cushion tomorrow, I want to see it in the dust." He took a deep breath, and h-he said, "You're on, bro. You're on. You bring it." The following morning, on the way to the cathedral of Santa Fe, my parents and I stopped at the . . . holy chapel of Chimayó and picked up the dirt from the Papu, the little hole where the holy dirt is. We wrapped it in a purificator and I told Fr. Conran [Runnebaum] who was co-officiating that day that this was to be put under his chin at the moment of consecration. Sure enough, he was brought in . . . the . . . up the nave, laid in cruciform in front of the cathedral and just as his chin was to be put on a silken cushion, I had it whisked away and motioned for Fr. Conran to open the purificator. He opened the purificator and there was the holy dirt of Chimayó and he . . . his chin rested on it. And he turned and he looked at me. I told him that if he was to serve the people of New Mexico, I wanted to see his face in the dust at the moment of his highest glory. Well, as they prayed the litany of the saints over him, suddenly the cathedral bell began to ring and it struck eleven, and he looked at me, startled. And I could see that he was ver . . . virtua . . . he was really disconcerted because the same thought was running through both of our minds. I had always told him that even at the eleventh hour, a man might come to glory. A . . . nd . . . he closed his eyes and I went outside and I wept. I don't know why.

Well, he became the priest of Abiquiu, which was the birthplace of the great Padre Martínez of Taos. And he was to serve there for six years and practice humility, which is not easy for him, no easier for him than it would be for me. In fact, when he would a . . . pray before the cruz, the cross of, the Aragon cross that we have hanging over our altar, he would say, "Make me worthy . . . Make me worthy . . . Make me worthy." And I would come up behind him and say, "Not even close, keep praying." [We both laughed.] I was so mean to him, but my job was to get him prepared for the priesthood. Well, he had always told me that one of the roles that he longed to play as an actor had always been that of Damien the Leper, which hadn't been portrayed on stage yet. Now it has, of course, many times. So he was going to write a manuscript for it and he gave me all his old manuscripts. I still have all the old manuscripts to the original productions he did here in New Mexico. So when I decided that Damien the Leper was to be . . . presented . . . I had painted—on the cupboard—I painted his face on it, so when you look at Damien the Leper with all his leprous . . . skin falling off, it's really José Rodriguez, [DM: um.] my friend, the actor who is head of that particular thing. When I went to his funeral—he died—[. . .] he was to . . . known to be a drug user when he was a . . . before his priestly days, when he was still an actor. And his ashes were brought into the church—all during Mass I kept weeping uncontrollably and my friend Michelle said a, "Do you miss him?" And I said "Yeah, kinda, but I'm just . . . crying because the choir is soooo bad." [Larry laughed—then I laughed.] Then I started laughing. I just needed it. I needed some kind of release. We went outside of the church. There had been a hole dug with a posthole digger and his ashes were dumped inside. Just then I noticed that all the theatre company from Albuquerque had come to see him. I walked up to the director or she walked up to me, the director of the theater company, Margarita Martínez, and she started pounding on my chest and saying, "You took him from us. You *took him* from us." And I said, "Nooo, I don't have that power." I said, "The Lord took him from us. He needed a comedian up in heaven." I said, "It was just ready for time. I just made the transition easier for him—from st . . . one stage to another." Wellll, he was gone. But he still lives on in the cupboard. And getting back to the cupboard. [. . .]

And on the final wall, right over the bed is the whole story of fear in northern New Mexico that is called Cocas y Coconas, or the Bogey Creatures of the Hispanic Southwest. I went to forty-two or forty-seven different villages and I asked them for, to tell me what the face of fear was in their village and to help me draw it and I would draw it and they'd say, "No, no, not like this—like this." Or, "Yeah, yeah—you're doing fine." And they would identify it for me. I thought it was very important in the history of New Mexico to unmask the bogeyman because so long as you do not unmask the bogeyman, he tends to have power over you. But if you can identify what the bogeyman does or what it represents then there is no longer reason to fear. So I re-created this children's book on the Spanish monsters of the

Southwest and gave it to various elementary schools so the kids can study it, color it, tear it apart, and it hath no domain over them, as it were. Also located in that bedroom is the statue of death that we have talked about, but here she is dressed in all her finery, and she is called Catrina. She's all dressed up and no one to take with her, no one to take her out dancing. It's one of my favorite rooms in the house. It's certainly a . . . someplace where guests can stay and a . . . enjoy it. Then of course you have the bathrooms, which have a little art, just poster work that I had done for the Mariachis Spectacular in Albuquerque or I'd put up a dragon above the shower area. I like the idea of being seen by a terrible dragon as I am showering.

[. . .] We'll talk about the steps leading toward the bedroom. You see six huge canvas pieces that are up there. The one closest to the bedroom door, shows me lying in my bed, surrounded by all my nightmares, all the things that go bump in the night. It was important that these things be painted; that they be researched, not only because they are part of the patrimony of fear that we had, but also because of the painting I was able to let go of a lot of hurts and a lot of pa . . . a lot of my childhood. I hardly look at them anymore, because they have su . . . become such an integral part of what I am. Somebody once said, "Boy, you must have a great imagination to have created all these." The answer was, even if I could, I wo . . . I couldn't have done it myself. I am not that talented. I am not that . . . that . . . that gifted to have created all these things. These are created by the culture. All I do is record what was created by the culture.

Right next to that there is another huge piece which has my coffin and my coffin . . . on my coffin I inscribed the words "era y soy polvo." "I was and I am dust." I thought it was a wonderful thing to put on my coffin and it, there are seven different grotesque figures. Of course, the biggest is San. Sebastiana herself; she is lady death. And then she is followed by . . . on one side, she is flanked on the left by the lady of the ax. That is another aspect of death. And then on the other side . . . is the . . . lady who's carrying, "what was it?" The lady of the ax . . . then there's a horrifying death next to her and then there is a prodigious death next to her; there's the joyful death next to her. There are a couple of ones that I can't remember but it shows you that Spanish do not take death for granted. The idea that there are seven different forms of death because death is not just death is not just death. How you die is just as important as how you live. And so . . . sometimes death can be very tragic, sometimes it can be faminous, sometimes it can be absolutely beautiful—like at the end of a long happy life, where you have made peace and it's just time to let go. [. . .]

[Larry is talking about the painting above his bed, which is about the Pueblo rebellion, 1680.] When news of the Great Massacre occurred at the Pueblo rebellion, bells were rung in Santa Fe and in Mexico City and as far away as Lima, Peru, in honor of the martyrs of the people who were killed. In fact we still have a . . . a street that runs next to my office here called Martyrs Lane that recalls that particular episode. The settlers were not to come back for another thirteen years, until 1693 with Oñate and try to resettle, this time a little of their arrogance and bravado was gone and they treated the Indians a little bit better. But it was certainly one of the darkest days of our history and . . . some people remark that it is such a violent scene for one to have over their bed. But I think . . . that only in being reminded of it can we let it go eventually and a . . . move forward.

The other great treasure in that room, which I rarely ever talk about because I'm always afraid that it will disappear is there are five icons there, five wooden panels and a Christ on a cross that were dug out of an old church in a Pueblo village. And the Indians of that area immediately wanted to destroy them all. Fr. Conran [Runnebaum], who was taking care of that village at that time sent to me, sent them to me, and he said, "Find out the secret of these icons." Now I know that sometimes we can take our icons, our retableaux, our Spanish wooden panels and plaster them into the walls as a punishment when a saint does not do what you want it to do . . . you put them on time out, basically . . . until he does what you want him to do. And then what you do is after you have gotten the favor, you remove him, you have him disimmured, cause he . . . you had him immured originally and then you put little offerings of food in front of them. Sometimes when God becomes a little too abstract you deal with the saints, with his intercessors. But what bothered me is that the Christ, the Christ on the cross, which is really no more than three hundred years old . . . it's an easy piece, though what's interesting is that I was curious as to why anybody would immure a Christ? Saints, yes. Christ, never. Not only that, somebody had been looking for something . . . [Larry answered the phone.] What bothered me was that somebody had taken great pains to look for something because all of the [. . .] gesso work that covered the rude carving of the Christ, had been removed, except for the head part. Nobody had touched the head part. Well, as I was holding one end of the cross, I suddenly dropped it. And it was probably the happiest accident of my life. Because, as I did, the corpus came off the Christ, off the cross and I found that it was hollow inside, from the back and inside the hollowed out chest, I found a little pouch. And inside that little pouch is a tiny little scroll with little Hebrew characters in it. That is called a mezuzah. What was apparently happening is that the crypto-Jews of that village were pretending to pray to the Jesus while really acknowledging the mezuzah inside the chest cavity. It is a wonderful, rare piece and people have been coming to look at it. I'm afraid that I need to have put some security around it eventually, maybe with another little plastic box that is anchored to the wall eventually because that really is the only proof we have in northern New Mexico that crypto-Jews existed over here and that's how they existed outside of Catholic circles. The only other room that is attached. [. . .]

[. . .] Also, prominent among that collection are eleven out of twelve paintings, since somebody stole one of them when it was hanging at the school . . . called the Fetus Sandwich Collection. There is fetus sandwiches which I said, fetuses and skulls seem to have a great deal of symbolism for me. This particular one I had been . . . at the museum of El Prado in Spain and had spent about six hours staring at the old classical piece where Father Time is chewing on his children, based on the old myth that time devours all things. And I had a dream that night, literally, I dreamed up that whole collection called what would happen if we were devouring our children these days. Because children are so abused and so neglected and so I literally dreamed up the fetus sandwich collection so that you'll have things like a . . . oh, you'll have a fetus wrapped in a tortilla, called a fetus burrito with guacamole on the side. It's what I call social surrealism; I think I am the only one who has ever done this. You'll find another one which is a pita fetus, with a red, white, and blue flag under it. Ah . . . then you have a fetus kabobs on a grill . . . you'll find a fetus with caviar and vodka. You'll find a fetus with roses and watermelon for Valentine's day . . . You'll find a one which is a . . . a fetus with an Italian bread with hard cooked egg and shrimp on the side. And there is one which is a fetus bagel with pickle on the side on an orange-and-blue-checkered tablecloth. All these things just trying to come up with some kind of internationality for all of these things. And the basic message is "stop destroying the children." Or, "we are destroying the children." Yeah . . . of themselves, they look kind of tongue-and-cheek or humorous, but really I think that they are probably amongst my m . . . amongst my most serious work. I think children are so vulnerable and so abused in so many ways and there is nobody there to advocate for them, in a very real sense from day to day. And even though it's very abstract, perhaps, they'll be understood. All my students seem to understand them. In fact they wanted me to make them into posters or into calendars so they could hang them up . . . complete with recipes there, don't you know. I never did. But those are the hidden treasures. Other things that are hidden in the house: there are fifteen posts that make up part of the railing on the staircase. Each of them is a time capsule, with something sealed within. I have probably the best archives of northern New Mexico so I seal what I think are the most important documents, so that eventually, maybe somebody will unearth them and understand what was going on in my mind as I was building this staircase of the house. And I think we're going to stop right there for now.

Appendix 4

Larry's Picture Book[1]

[1] The illustrations and commentary on the following four pages are taken from Larry's coloring/picture book: *Los cocos y las coconas: Bogey Creatures of the Hispanic Southwest*. Used with permission.

El Abuelo

El día 12 de diciembre, cuando la Fiesta de Nuestra Señora de Guadalupe se ha pasado, la gente de Nuevo México enciende *luminarias* para despertar a los *Abuelos*. Los Abuelos son espíritus ancestrales navideños de la gente. Despiertan de su *sueño anual* en las cuevas de las sierras. Bajan con sus *chicotes* y sacos para asegurar de que la gente no haya olvidado sus costumbres, oraciones y tradiciones. Se calientan alrededor de las luminarias y *farolitos* y bailan el jorundundú. Los Abuelos del invierno son buenos. Éstos vienen a instruír a la gente en la cultura. Pero si los muchachitos ven a un Abuelo en el verano, ¡cuidado! Esos son malos porque han despertado antes del tiempo de la Navidad y todavía tienen sueño. Ellos vienen a llevarse a los muchachitos *malcriados* para la sierra en sus sacos.

On the 12th of December, after the Feast of Our Lady of Guadalupe, the people of New Mexico light bonfires to awaken the Christmas Ogres. The Ogres are ancestral Christmas spirits that awaken from their year-long sleep in the caves in the mountains. They come down with whips and sacks to make sure that the people have not forgotten their customs, prayers and traditions. They warm themselves around the bonfires and Christmas lanterns and do a dance call the jornundundú. The Christmas Ogres that come in the wintertime are good. They come to teach the people about their culture. But if the children see a Christmas Ogre in the summertime, watch out! These Ogres are mean because they have awakened from their sleep before it's Christmas and they're still grouchy. They come to carry away naughty children in their sacks up to the mountains.

(Find the words in the English text that go with the following Spanish words:)

1. luminarias:
2. Abuelos:
3. sueño anual:
4. chicotes:
5. farolitos:
6. cuidado:
7. malcriados:

La Llorona

La Llorona es una mujer que llora por sus niños muertos. En 1519, Don Hernán Cortez fue a México y con la ayuda de la india Malinche, conquistó el imperio azteca. Malinche, también llamada Doña Marina por los españoles, reveló todos los secretos de los aztecas a Cortez porque lo amaba. Según la *leyenda*, Cortez, tuvo dos hijos con ella y después de conquistar México, regresó a España, abandonándola a ella y a sus hijitos *mestizos*. Como los niños no eran de sangre pura española, ni de sangre pura *indígena*, nadie los quería. *Enfurecida*, contra Hernán Cortez, Malinche mató a sus hijos y los echó en un lago. Después cuando murió y fue al Cielo, San Pedro le preguntó por sus hijos. Cuando supo que los había dejado en un *lago* muertos, San Pedro la obligó a regresar al mundo a buscarlos. Cuando Malinche, ahora la Llorona, halla a niños *al filo de* una acequia, río o lago, los abraza pensando que son los suyos. Cuando halla que no lo son, enfurecida, los ahoga.

La Llorona is a woman who weeps for her dead children. In 1519, Don Hernan Cortez went to Mexico and with the help of the Indian woman Malinche, conquered the Aztec empire. Malinche, also known as Doña Marina by the Spanish, revealed all of the secrets of the Aztecs to Cortez because she loved him. According to the legend, Cortez had two sons with her and after having conquered Mexico, he returned to Spain, abandoning her and his two mixed-blood children. Since the children were neither of pure Spanish blood nor or pure Indian blood, no one wanted them. Furious at Hernan Cortez, Malinche killed her children and threw them into a lake. Afterwards, when she died and went to Heaven, Saint Peter asked her for her children. When he learned that she had left them dead in a lake, Saint Peter sent her back to Earth to look for them. Whenever Malinche, now known as La Llorona, finds children at the edge of a ditch, river or lake, she hugs them thinking that they might be her own. When she finds that they are not hers, angrily, she drowns them!

(Find the words in the English text that go with the following Spanish words:)

1. La Llorona
2. leyenda:
3. mestizos:
4. indígena:
5. enfurecida:
6. lago:
7. al filo de:

Select Bibliography

Abu-Lughod, Lila. *Writing Women's Worlds: Bedouin Stories.* Berkeley: University of California Press, 1993.

Anderson, E. Byron, and Bruce T. Morrill, eds. *Liturgy and the Moral Self: Humanity at Full Stretch before God: Essays in Honor of Don E. Saliers.* Collegeville, MN: Liturgical Press, 1998.

Asad, Talal. *Genealogies of Religion: Discipline and Reasons of Power in Christianity and Islam.* Baltimore, MD: Johns Hopkins University Press, 1993.

Atkinson, Paul, and Martyn Hammersley. "Ethnography and Participant Observation." In *Handbook of Qualitative Research,* edited by Norman K. Denzin and Yvonna S. Lincoln. Thousand Oaks, CA: SAGE Publications, 1994.

Bell, Catherine. *Ritual Theory, Ritual Practice.* New York: Oxford University Press, 1992.

Benavides, Gustavo. "Resistance and Accommodation in Latin American Popular Religiosity." In *An Enduring Flame: Studies on Latino Popular Religiosity,* edited by Anthony M. Stevens-Arroyo and Ana María Díaz-Stevens. PARAL Studies Series 1. New York: Bildner Center for Western Hemisphere Studies, 1994.

Brown, Karen McCarthy. *Mama Lola: A Vodou Priestess in Brooklyn.* Berkeley: University of California Press, 1991.

Bull, James C. *Out of Time: Arroyo Seco: An Historic Look at a 250 Year Old Northern New Mexico Village.* Taos, NM: Wolff Publishing Co., 1998.

Carroll, Michael P. *The Penitente Brotherhood: Patriarchy and Hispano-Catholicism in New Mexico.* Baltimore, MD: Johns Hopkins University Press, 2002.

Chávez, Fray Angélico. *But Time and Chance: The Story of Padre Martínez of Taos, 1793–1867.* Santa Fe, NM: Sunstone Press, 1981.

———. *My Penitente Land: Reflections on Spanish New Mexico.* 1974. Reprint, Santa Fe: Museum of New Mexico Press, 1993.

Darley, Alex M. *The Passionists of the Southwest or the Holy Brotherhood: A Revelation of the 'Penitentes.'* 1893. Reprint, Glorieta, NM: Rio Grande Press, 1968.

De Aragon, Ray John. *Hermanos de la Luz: Brothers of the Light.* Santa Fe, NM: Heartsfire Books, 1998.

Díaz-Stevens, Ana María. "Analyzing Popular Religiosity for Socio-religious Meaning." In *An Enduring Flame: Studies on Latino Popular Religiosity,* edited by Anthony M. Stevens-Arroyo and Ana María Díaz-Stevens. PARAL Studies Series 1. New York: Bildner Center for Western Hemisphere Studies, 1994.

Dillon, Michele. *Catholic Identity: Balancing Reason, Faith, and Power*. New York: Cambridge University Press, 1999.

Elizondo, Virgilio P. "Popular Religion as Support of Identity." In *Mestizo Worship: A Pastoral Approach to Liturgical Ministry*, edited by Virgilio P. Elizondo and Timothy M. Matovina. Collegeville, MN: Liturgical Press, 1998.

En Divina Luz. Colores: Exploring the Myth and Magic of the American Southwest. KNME TV 5. Albuquerque, 1996.

Espín, Orlando O. "Popular Catholicism: Alienation or Hope?" In *Hispanic/Latino Theology: Challenge and Promise*, edited by Ada María Isasi-Díaz and Fernando F. Segovia. Minneapolis, MN: Fortress Press, 1996.

Fink, Peter E. *The New Dictionary of Sacramental Theology*. Collegeville, MN: Liturgical Press, Michael Glazier, 1990.

Grimes, Ronald L., ed. *Readings in Ritual Studies*. Upper Saddle River, NJ: Prentice-Hall, 1996.

———. *Symbol and Conquest: Public Ritual and Drama in Santa Fe*. Albuquerque: University of New Mexico Press, 1992.

Henderson, Alice Corbin. *Brothers of Light: The Penitentes of the Southwest*. 1937. Reprint, Las Cruces, NM: Yucca Tree Press, 1998.

Jenkins, Myra Ellen, and Albert H. Schroeder. *A Brief History of New Mexico*. Albuquerque: University of New Mexico Press, 1974.

Kavanagh, Aidan. *On Liturgical Theology: The Hale Memorial Lectures of Seabury-Western Theological Seminary, 1981*. Collegeville, MN: Liturgical Press, 1984.

Krieger, Susan. *Social Science and the Self: Personal Essays on an Art Form*. New Brunswick, NJ: Rutgers University Press, 1991.

Lakoff, George, and Mark Johnson. *Metaphors We Live By*. 1980. Reprint, Chicago, IL: University of Chicago Press, 2003.

The Lash of the Penitentes. VHS. Directed by Roland Price and Harry Revier. 35 min. Talisman Studios, 1936.

Lathrop, Gordon. *Holy Things: A Liturgical Theology*. Minneapolis, MN: Fortress Press, 1993.

Lawless, Elaine J. *Handmaidens of the Lord: Pentecostal Women Preachers and Traditional Religion*. Philadelphia: University of Pennsylvania Press, 1988.

———. *Holy Women, Wholly Women: Sharing Ministries through Life Stories and Reciprocal Ethnography*. Philadelphia: University of Pennsylvania Press, 1993.

Lofland, John, and Lyn H. Lofland. *Analyzing Social Settings: A Guide to Qualitative Observation and Analysis*. 3rd ed. Washington, DC: Wadsworths Publishing Co., 1995.

López Pulido, Alberto. *The Sacred World of the Penitentes*. Washington, DC: Smithsonian Institution Press, 2000.

Maduro, Otto. "Notes Toward a Sociology of Latina/o Religious Empowerment." In *Hispanic/Latino Theology: Challenge and Promise*, edited by Ada María Isasi-Díaz and Fernando F. Segovia. Minneapolis, MN: Fortress Press, 1996.

Mahan, Brian J. *Forgetting Ourselves on Purpose: Vocation and the Ethics of Ambition*. San Francisco, CA: Jossey-Bass, 2002.

McDannell, Colleen. *Material Christianity: Religion and Popular Culture in America*. New Haven, CT: Yale University Press, 1995.

Millicent Rogers Museum. *Padre Martinez: New Perspectives from Taos*. Taos, NM: Millicent Rogers Museum, 1988.

Mitchell, Nathan D. *Liturgy and the Social Sciences: American Essays in Liturgy*. Collegeville, MN: Liturgical Press, 1999.

———. "Revisiting the Roots of Ritual." *Liturgy Digest* 1, no. 1 (Spring 1993): 4–36.

Moschella, Mary Clark. *Ethnography as a Pastoral Practice: An Introduction*. Cleveland, OH: Pilgrim Press, 2008.

Orsi, Robert A. *Between Heaven and Earth: The Religious Worlds People Make and the Scholars Who Study Them*. Princeton, NJ: Princeton University Press, 2005.

———. "'Have You Ever Prayed to Saint Jude?': Reflections on Fieldwork in Catholic Chicago." In *Reimagining Denominationalism: Interpretive Essays*, edited by Robert Bruce Mullin and Russell E. Richey. New York: Oxford University Press, 1994.

———. "'He Keeps Me Going': Women's Devotion to Saint Jude Thaddeus and the Dialectics of Gender in American Catholicism." In *Belief in History: Innovative Approaches to European and American Religion*, edited by Thomas Kselman. Notre Dame, IN: University of Notre Dame, 1991.

———. "'Mildred, Is It Fun to Be a Cripple?': The Culture of Suffering in Mid-twentieth-century American Catholicism." *The South Atlantic Quarterly* 93, no. 3 (Summer 1994): 547–90.

———. *Thank You, St. Jude: Women's Devotion to the Patron Saint of Hopeless Causes*. New Haven, CT: Yale University Press, 1996.

Rebolledo, Tey Diana. *Women's Tales from the New Mexico WPA: La Diabla a Pie*. Houston, TX: Arte Público Press, 2000.

Rodriquez, Jeanette. *Our Lady of Guadalupe: Faith and Empowerment among Mexican-American Women*. Austin: University of Texas Press, 1994.

Rudnick, Lois Palken. *Utopian Vistas: The Mable Dodge Luhan House and the American Counterculture*. Albuquerque: University of New Mexico Press, 1996.

Schmemann, Alexander. *Introduction to Liturgical Theology*. Translated by Asheleigh E. Moorehouse. 1966. Reprint, Crestwood, NY: St. Vladimir's Seminary Press, 1996.

Sheehan, Michael J., ed. *Four Hundred Years of Faith, Seeds of Struggle—Harvest of Faith: A History of the Catholic Church in New Mexico*. Santa Fe, NM: Archdiocese of Santa Fe, 1998.

Stake, E. Robert. "Case Studies." In *Handbook of Qualitative Research*, edited by Norman K. Denzin and Yvonna S. Lincoln. Thousand Oaks, CA: SAGE Publications, 1994.

Steele, Thomas J., ed. and trans. *Archbishop Lamy: In His Own Words*. Albuquerque, NM: LPD Press, 2000.

———. *Santos and Saints: The Religious Folk Art of Hispanic New Mexico*. Santa Fe, NM: Ancient City Press, 1994.

Tate, Bill. *The Penitentes of the Sangre de Cristos: An American Tragedy*. A Tate Gallery Production. First Edition. Espanola, NM: The Rio Grande SUN, 1966.

Torres, Larry. *Los Cocos y las Coconas: Bogey Creatures of the Hispanic Southwest*. Arroyo Seco, NM: Larry Torres, 1995.

———. *Los Matachines Desenmascarados: An Historical Interpretation of the Ancient Dance-drama*. Arroyo Seco, NM: Larry Torres, 1996.

———, trans. *Six Nuevomexicano Folk Dramas for Advent Season*. Albuquerque: University of New Mexico Press, 1999.

Udell, Isaac L. *The Penitentes*. Denver, CO: Cosmopolitan Art Gallery, 1950.

Wallis, Michael, and Craig Varjabedian. *En Divina Luz: The Penitente Moradas of New Mexico*. Albuquerque: University of New Mexico Press, 1994.

Weigle, Marta. *Brothers of Light, Brothers of Blood: The Penitentes of the Southwest*. Santa Fe, NM: Ancient City Press, 1976.

———. *A Penitente Bibliography*. Albuquerque: University of New Mexico Press, 1976.

———. *The Penitentes of the Southwest*. Santa Fe, NM: Ancient City Press, 1970.

Writers' Program of the Work Projects Administration in the State of New Mexico. *New Mexico: A Guide to the Colorful State*. 1940. Reprint, Albuquerque: University of New Mexico Press, 1945.

———. *The WPA Guide to 1930s New Mexico*. 1940. Reprint, Tucson: The University of Arizona Press, 1989.

Wroth, William. *Images of Penance, Images of Mercy: Southwestern Santos in the Late Nineteenth Century*. Norman: University of Oklahoma Press, 1991.

Index

Abu-Lughod, Lila, 109
alabados, 12, 45–47, 50–51, 61,
    117–19
Anthony of the Desert, 93, 118
Anza, Juan Bautista de, 26
Aragon, Ray John de, 13
Archdiocese of Santa Fe, 14, 17, 30,
    32, 36
Archibeque, Don Miguel, 36
Arroyo Hondo, 14, 47, 92, 115–16,
    141
Arroyo Seco, vii, 3, 11–16
Asad, Talal, 95–100, 104–5
Ash Wednesday, 12, 43–44, 68, 87
Auxiliadoras, 13, 16–17, 41, 43, 46,
    48–49, 51, 53, 55, 57, 60, 108

Benedict, St., 93, 118
bogey creatures, 20, 68, 84, 144,
    149–53
bultos, 14
Byrne, Archbishop Edwin Vincent,
    36–37, 62, 141

Calvario (Calvary), 47, 170
Chávez, Fray Angélico, 13, 32, 92
Chávez, Rev. Vincent P., xii, xvi, 14,
    23, 26, 28, 35–36, 60–62, 67, 102,
    108
Chimayó, New Mexico, 82–83, 128,
    142–43
cofradías (confraternities), 3, 30, 92
Colonias, Las, New Mexico, 14, 47
confession, 98
confraternities, see cofradías
Conquistadora, La, 25
Constitution on the Liturgy, 2, 6

Corbin Henderson, Alice, 13
Coronado, Francisco Vásquez de, 24
Covington, Daniel, 7
cruelty, 56, 133
crypto-Jews, 147
Cuerno Verde, 26

Darley, Alex M., 13, 30, 34–35
disciplina, (whip), xi, 42, 95, 99
Divine Mercy, 8, 48, 107
Dodge, Mabel, 73, 77
Durango, Diocese of, 25, 27, 29, 37
dust/dirt, xii, 51, 56–57, 67, 79–80,
    83–89, 99, 101–3, 105, 113, 138,
    143, 145

Encuentro, El, see El Sermón del
    Encuentro de María Santísima
    con Su Amado Hijo
Erikson, Eric, 8
ethnography, xv–xvi, 70, 91, 109, 111

farolitos, 11, 124
flagellation, (whipping), vii, xi–xiii,
    7, 11–12, 28, 33, 42, 47, 60–61, 69,
    78–79, 87, 95, 99–100, 103, 106,
    138
forgiveness, 22, 78, 89, 98–99, 137
Foucault, Michel, 97
Francis, St., 32–34, 37, 93, 118
Franciscans (St. Francis Order, Third
    Order), 10, 25, 18, 34, 36, 92, 118,
    127
fury, 56

Gerken, Archbishop Rudolph
    Aloysius, 36

Godoy, Diego Lucero de, 25–26
Good Friday, 12–13, 28, 41–44, 47–50,
    60–61, 64, 67, 77–78, 87, 92, 104,
    116, 127, 137

Hermano Mama, 76, 136
Hermano Supremo Arzobispal, 36
Holy Trinity Parish, xvi, 14, 16,
    21–22, 27, 44, 47, 67, 115–17, 123,
    130
Holy Week, vii, 11–12, 15–18, 22, 28,
    39, 41–65, 67, 104
humility, 23, 83, 96–100, 104–5, 143

indigenous development theory,
    91–94
interviews, 7, 15, 17, 67, 69–70, 74,
    110, 112

Katholieke Universiteit Leuven, 1,
    112
Kavanagh, Aidan, vii, 4–5, 9, 18,
    105–8, 113
Kloss, Gene, 22

Lamy, Archbishop Jean Baptiste,
    21–23, 30–34, 38–39, 75, 92, 94,
    118, 140
late transplant theory, 91–92
Lawless, Elaine, 109–11
Leo XIII, Pope, 32
life stories, 3, 7, 11, 15, 17–20, 74–75,
    89, 102, 111–12, 131
lumen Christi, 78, 137
luminarias, 116, 119, 121

Madre Cuidadora, 43, 51, 55, 57, 61
Mahan, Brian, xv, 95–103
Martínez of Taos, Padre Antonio
    José, 23, 28, 32, 37, 75, 83, 101,
    118, 139–41, 143
Masons, 36
Matachines, los, 68, 74–75

mayordomos, 117
McCarthy Brown, Karen, 109
Mesa Directiva, 17, 31, 42, 62, 72, 101
Mitchell, Nathan, 105
morada, vii, 3, 11–22, 30–31, 33,
    35–36, 39, 41–51, 59–61, 63,
    65, 68, 76–77, 79, 86–87, 93, 95,
    100–101, 108–9, 123, 126–27, 130,
    136–37

Nuestra Señora de los Dolores, 3, 14,
    16, 19, 47, 51, 55, 59, 92, 115–17

obedience, 30–31, 33, 92–96, 101
O'Keeffe, Georgia, 77, 88–89, 102,
    107, 137
Orsi, Robert, xv, 7, 9–10, 70, 109–11

Padre Jesús Nazareno, 3, 17, 33,
    42–60, 91
paños menores (underwear), xi, 42
papal medallion, 21–23, 38
participant observation, 3, 7, 15, 70,
    113
Penitentes (Hermanos, Hermandad),
    xi
Penitentismo, 77, 81, 84–86, 89, 94,
    100, 102, 104, 109–10, 137, 141
peregrinos (pilgrims), 47, 51, 55, 82,
    93, 108, 124–27, 142
pilgrims, see peregrinos
Piux IX, Pope, xii, 21–23, 32, 101, 118,
    134, 139
Popé, 24
posada, 58, 123, 130
Posadas, Las, 16, 19–20, 62–63, 73–74,
    93, 123–30
Price, Roland, 37
primary theology, vii, 4–7, 17, 19, 91,
    105, 111, 113
privacy/private, 14, 16, 24, 28–29,
    31–32, 35, 37–38, 45, 47, 60, 71
Prosper of Aquitane, 4

Pueblo Revolt, 24–26
Pulido, Alberto López, 33, 37, 92

reciprocal ethnography, 111
ritual of crucifixion, 167–68, 171–72
Rodríquez Jeanette, 7
rosary, xi, 2, 11, 49, 51, 60–61, 140

San Cristóbal, New Mexico, 14, 47,
    123–30
San Sebastiana, 85, 145
Santo Entierro, 49
Santo Niño, 14, 123, 128, 130
Schmemann, Alexander, 107
secondary theology, 106–7, 110, 113
Second Vatican Council, ix–xi, 2, 6, 22
secrecy/secrets, 12, 16, 71, 31–32, 35,
    37–38, 61, 69, 71, 112
self, issues of the, 78–81, 83–86,
    88–89, 94–105, 110–12, 132–39,
    145
Sermón de Dos y Tres Caídas, El, 48,
    51, 53, 56
Sermón del Encuentro de María
    Santísima con Su Amado Hijo,
    El, 13, 19, 41–44, 47–48, 50–51,
    56, 58, 60–65, 68, 71, 127
Starr, Miribai, 64,
Stations of the Cross, 12, 48, 60, 116,
    118

Steele, Thomas, 30, 92

Taos, 12–14, 16, 21–28, 32, 37, 43,
    60–61, 63, 68, 73, 75, 83, 101, 109,
    118, 132, 139–41, 143
Taos Pueblo, 24, 27, 61
Taylor, Carl N., 37
Tinieblas (Tenebrae), 49, 60, 77, 79,
    104, 127, 137
Torres, Larry T., xi, 67–89, 131–53

Udell, Isaac L., xvi, 12, 60, 167–74
underwear, see paños menores

Valdez, New Mexico, 14, 27, 47
Vargas Zapata Luján Ponce de León
    y Contreras, Don Diego de, 25
Verónicas, 13, 16–17, 43, 45–46, 49,
    51, 55, 57, 61–62, 108
votive candles, ix–xi

Weigle, Marta, 13–14, 29–37, 43
whip, see disciplina
whipping, see flagellation
Worgul, George S., 8
Wroth, William, 13, 28, 43, 91–92, 95

Zubiría y Escalante, Bishop José
    Antonio Laureano de, 27–32,
    37, 101

The Penitente Paintings by Isaac L. Udell

The thirteen paintings that follow in these pages were painted by Isaac L. Udell in the late 1930s and early 1940s. While attending to some of the medical needs of the Penitentes in Northern New Mexico, Udell received permission to witness the Penitente practices and to paint what he had seen and experienced. Although he did not originally intend to make the paintings public, he was persuaded to publish the collection with the Cosmopolitan Art Gallery in 1950 in a black-and-white gallery booklet. At the time of publication, Udell was pursuing his master's degree in the Department of Fine Arts at the University of Colorado. Still reticent about publishing the paintings, Udell writes, "I can ask only, at the expense of appearing sentimental, that the story of Penitente Brotherhood be received with understanding charity and humane kindness in return for a knowledge of a people whose heritage is rich in bravery and daring, whose faith is deep and unquestioning, and whose conviction is sure."[1] Along with each painting in the booklet Udell provides a brief commentary.

These paintings and their corresponding commentaries raise as many questions as they answer. As the reader will see, Udell portrays a Penitente crucifixion ritual in paintings 7 and 8. He describes painting 7, *Raising the Cross*, this way: "The ritual of the crucifixion varies slightly in the presentation from year to year and in the various communities, although essentially it is the same." He goes on to say that painting 7 portrays Penitente crucifixion in a smaller village that cannot sustain a "grand scale ceremony." Consequently, the crowd of witnesses, called the gallery, and the cross are smaller. In painting 8, however, the Penitente is securely bound to a larger cross. Udell declares that some of the subjects for crucifixion "cried out to be nailed rather than tied, but in the last few years nailing had been abandoned."

---

[1] Isaac L. Udell, *The Penitentes* (Denver, CO: Cosmopolitan Art Gallery, 1950).

The crucifixion subject was left on the cross for several minutes, until he lost consciousness. Often he was injured. Sometimes the Penitente died from the practice. If that happened, the Brothers would simply announce the death to the family by placing an article of clothing on their doorstep, which is depicted in painting 12.

If the Hermandad had not been forced by the authorities of the Roman Catholic Church to keep their practices secret, these paintings could be used as part of a larger ethnographic study. My access to the testimonies of these paintings assisted me in developing some of my questions for Larry. For example, in discussing the paintings depicting the crucifixion ritual Larry explained that this practice had been abandoned before he became a member.

1. *Official Seal of the Order*

2. Beginning the Procession

3. Penitente Procession

4. *Calvario/Calvary*

6. *Whippers at Night*

5. *Penitentes around the Cross*

7. *Raising the Cross*

8. *Penitente Crucifixion*

9. *Procession with Carreta de Muerto/Death Cart*

10. *Tinieblas/Tenebrae*

11. *Procession with Gallery*

12. *Death Came during Penance*

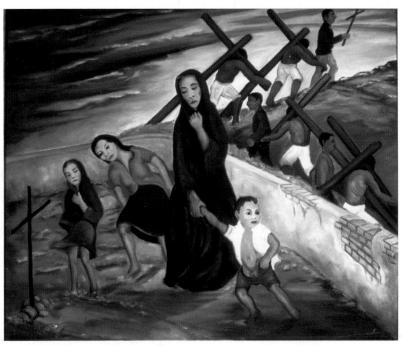

13. *The Last Cross*